Praise for *World of Wonders*

"Within two pages, nature
fresh and new. Nezhukuma
story about love, identity a
losing the language and the abi
the wondrous things ar
impoverished by this process. [. . .] This book demands we
find the eyes to see and the heart to love such things once
more. It is a very fine book indeed, truly full of wonder."
—*New York Times* Book Review

"From its gorgeous illustrations to its unusual combination
of lyrical nature writing and memoir, *World of Wonders* is
hands-down one of the most beautiful books of the year."
—NPR, "Best Books of 2020"

"In thirty bewitching essays, Nezhukumatathil spotlights
natural astonishments ranging from monsoon season in
India to clusters of fireflies in western New York, each one
a microcosm of joy and amazement. With her ecstatic prose
and her rapturous powers of insight, Nezhukumatathil
proves herself a worthy spiritual successor to the likes of
Mary Oliver and Annie Dillard, setting the bar high
for a new generation of nature writers."
—*Esquire*, "Best Books of 2020"

"Should the wonderful David Attenborough ever retire,
my hope is someone at BBC has read the work of Aimee
Nezhukumatathil. [. . .] What a lovely book this is, gentle in
its pacing, well-illustrated by Fumi Nakamura, and quietly
subversive in the way she channels its gusts of joy."
—Literary Hub

"*World of Wonders* is flabbergasted, gobsmacked, and
astonished with glee by all kinds of creatures and phenomena,
all kinds of kin, from flamingos to catalpas, from monsoons
to corpse flowers, from dancing frogs to axolotls."
—Ross Gay, *Poets & Writers*

NEW YORK TIMES BESTSELLER

PRAISE FOR *WORLD OF WONDERS*

"Nezhukumatathil's investigations, enhanced by Nakamura's vividly rendered full-color illustrations, range across the world, from a rapturous rendering of monsoon season in her father's native India to her formative years in Iowa, Kansas, and Arizona, where she learned from the native flora and fauna that it was common to be different. [. . .] The writing dazzles with the marvel of being fully alive."

—*Kirkus Reviews* (starred)

"Reading *World of Wonders*, it's clear that Nezhukumatathil is a poet. These essays sing with joy and longing—each focusing on a different natural wonder, all connected by the thread of Nezhukumatathil's curiosity and her identification with the world's beautiful oddities. [. . .] It's a heartwarming, poignant, and often funny collection, enlivened by Fumi Nakamura's dreamy illustrations."   —BuzzFeed, "Best Books of 2020"

"Each essay is a joyous reminder that the world we inhabit is not ours alone. This essay collection will make you look at the trees in your yard a bit tenderly, dig out some old photos, call your family, and maybe fill you with a bit more hope, resilience, and wonder."

—Vulture, "32 Books to Gift for the Holidays"

"This year, I'm giving everybody a copy of Aimee Nezhukumatathil's *World of Wonders* [. . .]. It's lyrical and surprising and I can't think of anyone who wouldn't love it as a gift, which is why I'm buying it in bulk."

—Amber Sparks, author of *And I Do Not Forgive You*, in the *Washington Post*'s "Which Books Make the Best Gifts?"

"A truly wondrous essay collection that reminds us that when we look close enough we can see that we are surrounded by extraordinary things."   —Roxane Gay, The Audacity

"These are the praise songs of a poet working brilliantly in prose. Each essay compresses a great deal of art and truth into a small space, whether about fireflies or flamingos, monkeys or monsoons, childhood or motherhood, or the trials and triumphs of living with a brown skin in a dominant white world. You will not find a more elegant, exuberant braiding of natural and personal history."
—Scott Russell Sanders, author of *The Way of Imagination*

"It can be helpful to focus on the wonder of the natural world when so much of what is happening around us feels out of our control. [. . .] *World of Wonders* urges us to take a breath and look around."   —NPR Morning Edition

"Lyrical sentences [that] display an abiding attention to what others might dismiss as strange."   —*Wall Street Journal*

"The nature writing we have been exposed to has been overwhelmingly male and white, which is just one reason that Aimee Nezhukumatathil's latest essay collection, *World of Wonders*, is a breath of fresh air. [. . .] What makes her work shine is its joyful embrace of difference, revealing that true beauty resides only in diversity." —*San Francisco Chronicle*

"[Nezhukumatathil's] kaleidoscopic observations pay off in these thoughtful, nuanced, surprise-filled essays. [. . .] Her book is a reminder not only of the power and beauty of the natural world, but of how we are inextricably a shaper of it, for better or worse."   —*Minneapolis Star Tribune*

"[These] gorgeous essays reveal how nature is both for all of us, and for each of us, deeply personal."   —*Garden & Gun*

"Brightly crafted microcosms of childhood, identity, belonging, parenthood, and memory. From fireflies recalling summer nights in rural western New York to touch-me-not plants sparking a contemplation on closeness, the writing shines with a tactile and beautiful lyricism that reimagines the world we see every day and sparks new magic in it."

—*Ralph Lauren Magazine*

"Aimee Nezhukumatathil sings praise and scours old wounds in this vivid and provocative essay collection. [. . .] Nature writing has largely been a white enterprise; however, Nezhukumatathil's point of view clears a path to redemption— one in which we acknowledge that we all belong (and are accountable) to each other as well as to this strange and wondrous Earth."

—Terrain.org

"Only a poet as talented as Aimee Nezhukumatathil could have written the essays in *World of Wonders*. This is prose that exhibits exquisite imagery and clear yet unexpected language, with a conclusion that arrives far too quickly. [. . .] Beyond the fascinating facts and distinctive imagery, and the touching stories that she tells, one is left with an unforgettable experience of the ephemerality of our environments, and the value in—the necessity of—standing still and looking around to marvel."

—*Rain Taxi*

"[This] shimmering essay collection about fantastic creatures and plants, *World of Wonders*, is shot through with memories of her peripatetic life and observations about race, motherhood, and environmental issues. [. . . It's] a bibliophilic and visual delight that dazzles the senses, much like Nezhukumatathil's beloved comb jellies. Her entrancing essays are a reminder to spend more time outdoors wondering at and cherishing this 'magnificent and wondrous planet.'"

—*Foreword Reviews* (starred)

"A lovely, thoughtful series of meditations, charmingly illustrated, with love and awe on every page but never shying away from the prickliness of life." —*Shelf Awareness*

Also by Aimee Nezhukumatathil

Oceanic
Lucky Fish
At the Drive-In Volcano
Miracle Fruit

WORLD OF WONDERS

In Praise of Fireflies,

Whale Sharks, and Other Astonishments

AIMEE NEZHUKUMATATHIL

with illustrations by

FUMI MINI NAKAMURA

MILKWEED EDITIONS

First paperback edition, published 2024 by Milkweed Editions
Printed in Canada
Cover design by Mary Austin Speaker
Cover and interior illustrations by Fumi Mini Nakamura
Author photo by Caroline Beffa
Illustrator photo by Silhouette Studio NYC
24 25 26 27 28   5 4 3 2 1

978-1-63955-056-2

Library of Congress Cataloging-in-Publication Data

Names: Nezhukumatathil, Aimee, author.
Title: World of wonders : in praise of whale sharks, fireflies, and other
    astonishments / Aimee Nezhukumatathil.
Description: First edition. | Minneapolis : Milkweed Editions, 2020. |
    Summary: "From beloved, award-winning poet Aimee Nezhukumatathil
    comes a debut work of nonfiction-a collection of essays about the
    natural world, and the way its inhabitants can teach, support, and
    inspire us"--
    Provided by publisher.
Identifiers: LCCN 2020010522 (print) | LCCN 2020010523 (ebook) | ISBN
    9781571313652 (hardcover) | ISBN 9781571319593 (ebook)
Subjects: LCSH: Animals--Anecdotes.
Classification: LCC QL791 .N425 2020 (print) | LCC QL791 (ebook) |
DDC
    590--dc23
LC record available at https://lccn.loc.gov/2020010522
LC ebook record available at https://lccn.loc.gov/2020010523

Milkweed Editions is committed to ecological stewardship. We strive to align our
book production practices with this principle, and to reduce the impact of our
operations in the environment. We are a member of the Green Press Initiative, a
nonprofit coalition of publishers, manufacturers, and authors working to protect
the world's endangered forests and conserve natural resources. *World of Wonders*
was printed on acid-free 100% postconsumer-waste paper by Friesens Corporation.

For my parents—
Paz and Mathew, my first wonders

CONTENTS

The butterfly counts not months but moments,
and has time enough.

—RABINDRANATH TAGORE

WORLD
OF
WONDERS

CATALPA TREE
Catalpa speciosa

A catalpa can give two brown girls in western Kansas a green umbrella from the sun. *Don't get too dark, too dark*, our mother would remind us as we ambled out into the relentless midwestern light. Every day after school, the bus dropped me and my younger sister off at Larned State Hospital, and every day, our classmates stared at us as the bus pulled away. I'd unlock the door to the doctor's quarters with a key tied to my yarn necklace and we'd go inside, fix ourselves snacks, and finish worksheets on fractions or spelling. We'd wait till our mom called to say we could meet her in her office, a call that meant she was about ten minutes away from being done for the day. We'd click off the TV and scramble to get our plastic jelly sandals on for the block-long walk to the hospital's administration building. Catalpa trees dotted the wide prairie grounds and watched over us as we made our way to Mom's office. My sister and I knew not to go anywhere near the fence line of the patients' residence because they sometimes were given basketball privileges outside, behind three layers of barbed wire. But occasionally I allowed myself to look at them when I rode my maroon three-speed bike, and sometimes an inmate would wave as I passed.

Catalpas stand as one of the largest deciduous trees at almost sixty feet tall, and dangle long bean pods and flat seeds with wings to help them fly. These bean pods inspire some to call the catalpa *cigar tree, trumpet creeper*, or *catawba*. Catalpa trees can help you record the wind as it claps their giant heart-shaped leaves together—leaves with spit curls, not unlike a naughty boy from a fifties movie, whose first drag race ends in defeat and spilled milkshakes. But these leaves can make a right riot of applause on a particularly breezy day. A catalpa planted too close to a house is a calamity just waiting to happen, but perhaps some people think the danger isn't too menacing since catalpas also yield good tone wood for guitars. And who would challenge that song out there on the plains?

All those songs call out to the sphinx moth, who lays about five hundred half-millimeter eggs at a time on the catalpa's leaves. These leaves are the moth's only source of food, and if left unchecked, the caterpillars can completely defoliate a single mighty tree. Kids in the Central Plains know these "worms" as good spending money. The sphinx caterpillars (also known as "catfish candy") make prized fishing bait; catfish and bluegill gobble them without seeming to get the least bit suspicious about their sudden appearance in the water.

Sometimes, before we left to pick up our mom, my sister and I gathered coins for the vending machine in the lobby of her office. In 1986, a Little Debbie brownie cost a precious thirty-five cents—precious because what little allowance we received was inconsistent, and so we couldn't count on it for gummy bracelets stacked up my arm in imitation of Madonna, or for the occasional ninety-nine-cent ice cream sandwich at Dairy Queen, or to save up for another colorful pair of jelly sandals. We were known as the daughters of the new doctor in that sleepy little county, but my mom made sure we weren't spoiled, unlike most of her coworkers' kids— children who had six or seven pairs of the latest high-tops, or were already talking about what luxury sports car would be their first. Extravagance, then, was the occasional afternoon when my sister and I found just enough to split a brownie between us.

After greeting the receptionist, riding the elevator up a few stories, and walking past the patients' pool tables and lounge, we'd greet our mother with bits of chocolate in our smiles. *Cavities, cavities!* she'd cluck at us, dropping whatever she was doing to hug and kiss us hello. I only pieced it together years later—how her day was spent trying to help patients who often hurled racist taunts and violent threats against her, like *Get out of here, Chink,* or *I'll choke you with my own hands!*

I can't believe how she managed the microaggressions of families who told her that they couldn't understand her accent, who spoke loud and slow at her, like she—the valedictorian of her class, the first *doctora* of her tiny village in northern Philippines—was a child who couldn't understand. But my mother always kept her calm, repeating recommendations and filing reports without losing her temper.

How did she manage to leave it all behind in that office, switching gears to listen to the ramblings of her fifth- and sixth-grade girls with their playground dramas, slights, and victories? I don't remember her talking about work while she walked home, changed out of her stylish suits, or fixed us hot meals from scratch. I only knew of what she regularly had to suffer because I'd sneak into and skim over her journals while she was in the shower or brushing her teeth. If not for those little peeks, I never would have known what she had to endure that year.

Thirty years later, I find myself underneath the largest catalpa tree in Mississippi. This tree is one of the centerpieces of the famous "tree walk" at the University of Mississippi, where I now teach. Its branches stretch horizontally to nearly the length of a bus, and have to be reinforced by metal supports in several areas so the branches that are soft and starting to get mushy at the center don't fall on an unsuspecting coed.

The foot-long leaves of catalpa trees like this one, for me, always meant shade from persistent sun and shelter from unblinking eyes. When I moved to the South, I thought I'd need to make use of those wide leaves constantly, but for the first time in my life, I haven't had to. And for the first time in their young lives, my kids see brown people other than me on a daily basis. Nobody stares at me here in the South. No one stares at my parents when they visit, or when they're at home now in central Florida. In their backyard, my parents spend their retirement crafting an elaborate garden, planting trees with much smaller leaves, and one of their great joys is to tend to the trees after a daily walk. To tug off any dead leaves or branches, pruning them just so, more orderly than any haircut they've ever given me. When I visit, one of my favorite things is to walk among the fruit trees with my mother while she regales me with all the tree-drama that's occurred since I was last there: *Can you believe all the flowers fell off this tree during the last hurricane? Too bad—no mangoes this year. Here is the tree where the vanda orchid grows best, remember? I told your father the birds are going to steal everything on this tree and he didn't listen, can you imagine?*

On campus, when I pass the giant catalpa tree, I think of that shy sixth grader who was so nervous when people stared. But then I remember the confident clickety-clack of my mother's heels as she walked home from work with me and my sister—when people would stare at us but my mother didn't seem to mind or notice. I remember her radiant smile when we burst through her office door, and then her laugh as she listened to our tales of the lunchroom and gym dramas of the day. I hear my own heels as I rush to meet my first class.

The campus catalpa offers up its creamy blossoms to the morning, already sultry and humid at nine o'clock in the morning. It still stands, even through the two or three tornado warnings we've had just this first windy year in Mississippi. As I pass the enormous tree, I make note of which leaves could cover my face entire if I ever needed them again. If I ever needed to be anonymous and shield myself from questions of *What are you?* and *Where are you from?* I keep walking. My students are waiting. My sweet southern students, who insist on calling me "Ma'am," no matter how much I gently protest. And I can't wait to see their beautiful faces.

FIREFLY
Photinus pyralis

When the first glimmer-pop of firefly light appears on a summer night, I always want to call my mother just to say hello. The bibliography of the firefly is a tender and electric dress, a small flame sputtering in the ditches along a highway, and the elytra covering the hind wings of the firefly lift like a light leather, suppler than any other beetle's. In flight, it is like a loud laugh, the kind that only appears in summer, with the stink of meats sizzling somewhere down the street, and the mouths of neighborhood children stained with popsicle juice and hinging open with the excitement of a ball game or tag.

I used to see fireflies as we drove home from family vacations, back to rural western New York. My father loved to commute through the night, to avoid the summer glare and heat. My sister and I would be wrapped in blankets, separated by a giant ice chest in the back seat, and I'd fall in and out of a sleep made all the more delicious by hearing the pleasant murmurings of my parents in the front. Sometimes I tried to listen, but looking out the car window, I'd always get distracted by the erratic flashes of light blurring past us.

For a couple of weeks every June, in the Great Smoky Mountains, the only species of synchronous firefly in North America converges for a flashy display. Years ago, my family stopped in this area during one of our epic road trips. My father knew to park our car away from the side of an impossibly verdant hill that plunged into a wide valley full of trillium, pin cherry, and hobblebush. He knew to cover our one flashlight with a red bag, so as not to disturb the fireflies, and to only point it at the ground as he led his wife and semi-aloof teenage daughters through the navy blue pause just moments after twilight. I confess, at first I wanted to be back in the air-conditioned hotel room—anywhere but on an isolated gravel path with the odd bullfrog clamor interrupting the dark. But now I think of my sister and I scattered in different homes as adults and am so grateful for all of those family vacations where we could be outdoors together, walking this earth.

My mother's temper was always frazzled by vacation's end, but I know each day off from work and spent with her family was something sweet and rare. How I crave those slow vacation days and even slower nights, her taking her time to select our frilled nightclothes, to laugh about the day's sightseeing and the cheap trinkets I'd bought. She'd pull a coverlet to my chin. Her gorgeous, dark and wavy hair tickled when she leaned over to kiss me good-night, smelling of Oil of Olay and spearmint gum. Only on those trips would I know such a degree of tenderness, the quiet reassurances a mother can give a daughter, while she stroked my bangs to the side of my face. No rush in the mornings to get me and my sister shuffled onto a school bus and herself off to work. When my mother is no longer here, I know I will cling to that lovely fragrance of mint and a moisturizer I'll always associate with beauty and love. I will cling to those summer nights we raced— and yet didn't race—home. I will try to bang myself back to that Oldsmobile like the lacewings that argue nightly with my porch light bulb, to what my small family was then, not even big enough to call a swarm: one sister, two parents.

I grew up near scientists who worked with indigo buntings. There is no other blue like that of these birds, no feather more electric. They navigate by following the North Star, and these scientists were trying to trick them into following a false star in a darkened room. But most of these buntings don't fall for the ruse. When released, they find their way home the same as always. The buntings know the North Star by heart, learn to look for it in their first summer of life, storing this knowledge to use years later when they first learn to migrate. How they must have spent hours gazing at the star during those nestling nights, peeking out from under their mother. What shines so strong holds them steady.

Where the buntings remain steadfast, fireflies are more easily deceived. They lose their light rhythm for a few minutes after a single car's headlights pass. Sometimes it takes hours for them to recalibrate their blinking patterns. What gets lost in the radio silence? What connections are translated incorrectly or missed entirely? Porch lights, trucks, buildings, and the harsh glow of streetlamps all complicate matters and discourage fireflies from sending out their love-light signals—meaning fewer firefly larvae are born the next year.

Scientists can't agree on how or why these fireflies achieve synchronicity. Perhaps it is a competition between males, who all want to be the first to send their signals across the valleys and manna grass. Perhaps if they all flash at once, the females can better determine whose glow is most radiant. Whatever the reason—and in spite of, or rather, because of, all the guided tours that now pop up in the Smokies—fireflies don't glow in sync all night long anymore. The patterns sometimes occur in short flashes, then abruptly end in haunting periods of darkness. The fireflies are still out there, but they fly or rest on grass blades in visual silence. Perhaps a visitor forgot to dim a flashlight or left their car lights on for too long, and this is the firefly's protest.

Firefly eggs and larvae are bioluminescent, and the larvae themselves hunt for prey. They can detect a slime trail from a slug or snail and follow it all the way to the juicy, unsuspecting source. Whole groups of larvae have been known to track relatively large prey, such as an earthworm—like a macabre, candlelit chase right out of an old B-movie, to the edge of a soupy pond, the larvae pulsing light as they devour a still-wriggling worm. Some firefly larvae live completely underwater, their lights fevering just under the surface as they capture and devour aquatic snails.

For a beetle, fireflies live long and full lives—around two years—though most of it is spent underground, gloriously eating and sleeping to their hearts' content. When we see these beacons flashing their lights, they usually have only one or two weeks left to live. Learning this as a child—I could often be found walking slowly around untrimmed lawns, stalling and not quite ready to go inside for dinner—made me melancholy, even in the face of their brilliance. I couldn't believe something so full of light would be gone so soon.

I know I will search for fireflies all the rest of my days, even though they dwindle a little bit more each year. I can't help it. They blink on and off, a lime glow to the summer night air, as if to say: *I am still here, you are still here, I am still here, you are still here, I am, you are,* over and over again. Perhaps I can will it to be true. Perhaps I can keep those summer nights with my family inside an empty jam jar, with holes poked in the lid, a twig and a few strands of grass tucked inside. And for those unimaginable nights in the future, when I know I'll miss my mother the most, I will let that jar's sweet glow serve as a night-light to cool and cut the air for me.

PEACOCK
Pavo cristatus

I'm eight and I've just returned from my first trip to southern India. During that time, I fell completely in love with peacocks—India's national bird—in spite of the strays in my grandparents' courtyard that shrieked every morning like cats being dragged over thumbtacks. Memories of those peacocks' turquoise and jade feathers and bright blue necks curl over my shoulder as I listen to my third-grade teacher announce an animal-drawing contest. My knees bounce at my desk. Of *course* I know what I'm going to draw.

We've just moved to suburban Phoenix from a small town in Iowa, where I was the only brown girl in my class. Although my new classmates stared hard at me when I was first introduced, I felt so happy to see kids of all shades in the room. I watch these classmates go off to the library to search for their animals, and ask my teacher if I can just stay and get started on my drawing. She fumbles in her purse and I see a pack of cigarettes. *No, you may not. We all need to be on the same page,* she says. In the library, I scan the shelves. There are no books on peacocks. My friends choose various dog breeds, small reptiles, kittens. In my notebook, I write in careful cursive, "Peacocks are the national bird of India." Then the bell rings and summons us back to class.

My teacher walks up and down the aisles, checking our work. When she stops at my desk, I smell and hear a smoky sigh, and her long maroon nail taps my notebook twice. I have no idea what this means. When it comes time to draw our animals on thick sheets of white construction paper, I begin with a sea of bright teal and purple. I outline the dramatic eye of the peacock in black, like he's wearing eyeliner. The rest of the page blooms with peacock feathers, dozens of violet eyes. I see the drawing the kid next to me is working on, a mostly blank page with a single squiggle on it: a snake.

My teacher continues to stalk through the rows of our desks. *Some of us misunderstood the assignment,* she says. She reaches the front of the room, and cleared her throat. *Some of us will have to start over and draw American animals. We live in Ah-mer-i-kah!* Now she looks right at me. My neck flushes. *Anyone who is finished can bring your drawing up to my desk and start your math worksheets. Aimee—* The class turns to look at me. *Looks like you need a do-over!*

I turn my drawing over and blink hard, trying not to let tears fall onto the page. Does she think peacocks can't live in this country? I saw peacocks at the San Diego Zoo the summer before, and my father once told me that roads are even blocked off for peacocks in Miami, where they can be seen strolling across lawns in the suburbs.

I pick up a new sheet of paper, slink back to my desk, and draw the most American thing I can think of: a bald eagle perched on a branch at the edge of a cliff, two eggs peeking up from its delicately balanced nest. I know the nest looks like a basket of Easter eggs, but I don't care anymore. I just want to be done so my classmates will stop staring. I color the wings with the saddest sepia crayon in my art supplies box. Before I turn the drawing in, I add an American flag—as big as the one hung outside our school—its pole poked into the tree's branches. Nothing about this drawing looks natural, especially since I drew the flag so much larger than the eagle's nest. Of course, I knew even then that eagle's nests are huge—about as wide and as tall as an elephant—but I didn't want her to ask me any more questions, so I just kept quiet.

When I get home that day, I park myself on the couch and stare at the television. When my dad calls me to dinner, I tell him I'm not hungry. When he walks into the living room to ask me to come to the dinner table anyway, I burst out, *Why do we need to have these* peacocks *all over the house? Wooden peacocks, brass peacocks, a peacock painting—it's so embarrassing!* My dad says nothing, just walks out of the room and gently calls back, *Your dinner will be cold.* But the next day, all the peacocks in the house are gone. *All* the peacocks, except for our family calendar: twelve months of peacocks—in front of a waterfall, a museum, a wall of bougainvillea; albino peacocks, peahens, and peachicks. That calendar remains, marking our time that year with its little squares and a new set of dramatic eyes looking back at me each month.

Weeks later, after announcements and the Pledge of Allegiance, my teacher declares the results of the drawing contest: my ridiculous, overly patriotic eagle drawing has won first place. It will be displayed in the giant glass trophy case right outside the principal's office. I will always hurry past it on my way to class.

I was a girl who loved to draw. I was a girl who loved color, who loved a fresh box of crayons, who always envied the girls with sixty-four colors but made do with my twenty-four off-brand shades. I was a girl who loved to draw— and yet, after that contest, I don't think I ever drew a bird again, not even a doodle, until well into adulthood.

This is the story of how I learned to ignore anything from India. The peacock feathers my grandfather had carefully collected for me the day before I left India grew dusty in the back of my closet instead of sitting in a vase on my white dresser. This is the story of how, for years, I pretended I hated the color blue. But what the peacock can do is remind you of a home you will run away from and run back to all your life: My favorite color is peacock blue. My favorite color is peacock blue. *My favorite color is peacock blue.*

COMB JELLY

Mertensia ovum

Who on earth would think to give solid glass bracelets to a four-year-old? My eyes were big as quarters when I opened the box of bangles sent by my Indian grandmother. She thought it was time. I loved them right away: the shock of color when I held my thin wrists up to the sunny window, the clink and chime when I ran, the deep-drenched reds, blues, violets—nothing else rang so bold or brilliant in a Chicago winter. Outside, drifts piled higher than a toddler in Moon Boots. My father shoveled snow off our roof for fear of a cave-in. But I had my bangles. I ran from room to room just to ring them. *Be careful, be careful*, my mother said. *You'll cut yourself if they break.*

And when I finally grew tired, I'd lie on the floor of our living room and listen for the strange sounds of winter: the scream of icicles as they slid off the edge of the gutters, the vermiculite in the cool soil of a houseplant begging for a drink. I held the bangles up to the ceiling light so I could fracture a rainbow across the room—so much power in a tiny bracelet of glass—the first time such radiance sprang from this little girl's hand.

As an adult, I'm still so drawn to light-soaked color displays. Some of the planet's most vibrant light shows come not from the land or air, but from the ocean. With the pulse and undulation of the comb jelly, hundreds of thousands of cilia flash mini-rainbows even in the darkest polar and tropical ocean zones. This zing of color is what tempts people all up and down the eastern coast of both Americas to gather walnut-sized comb jellies into their hands. But don't do this! Most are so delicate (thinner than the thinnest contact lens) that they will disintegrate in your palm. If you want to observe one up close, scoop it into a clear cup and take a look-see that way. And then, of course, please gently return it to the water.

The comb jelly is a creature of delicacy. It doesn't sting, and it's not actually a jellyfish. It belongs to a whole other phylum, *Ctenophora*. Comb jellies can be as small as a single grain of rice or they can grow to over four feet in width—large enough (in theory) to gobble up a plump second grader whole. But they won't, because they are too busy waving their hair-like cilia around, too busy eating various fish eggs, and too busy eating other comb jellies.

When I see them in aquariums, I think of the first time I held my glass bangles up to the light. I have always been drawn to color—the hue and cry of joy—and I think perhaps it was because someone on the other side of the planet entrusted those bangles, that fragility, to me when I was so young. What a waterworld comb jellies make, suspending their millions of rainbows not in the sky, but in the ocean—sometimes so far into the way-down deep and dazzle that only pale creatures like ang-lerfish and gulper eels take notice, perhaps imagining, for a brief moment, the delicious luxury of what it's like to be warmed by the sun after a rain.

TOUCH-ME-NOTS
Mimosa pudica

Of all the approximately 1.5 million plants the Chicago Botanic Garden has on site, the one that scared and delighted me the most when I was a child was *Mimosa pudica*—the touch-me-not plant. (Or, depending on your preference: sensitive plant, shame plant, humble plant, tickle-me plant, and my favorite, sleeping grass.) In Malayalam, my father's language, it's called *thottavadi*, which—if you are a wily second grader—is an especially fun name to call a shy goldfish or an orphaned bunny you find after school one day, or to simply scream out loud while riding a bike in the suburbs. Why all the fuss and euphoria over some greenery? Well, I still coo over its delightful pinnation, the double-leaf pattern feathering outward then inward from both sides of a single stem, and its spherical lavender-pink flowers, which bloom only in summer, and look as if someone crossed a My Little Pony doll with a tiny firework. But its best and most notable feature is that when you piano your fingers over the leaves of this plant, they give a shudder and a shake and quickly fold shut, like someone doesn't want to spill a secret.

Scientists have learned that when the plant's leaves are touched, potassium ions are released, causing a significant drop in cell pressure and leading the leaves to collapse as if the plant were nodding off to sleep. This elegant movement, called *thigmonasty*, topples carpenter worms and spider mites to the ground just as they think they'll be getting their bite on.

The touch-me-not is native to Central and South America but can be found along roadsides in Florida and as far north as Maryland. I've seen expensive grow kits for them in hobby and craft stores, which my parents find amusing; in India and the northern Philippines, the plant is often considered a weed. Woe to those who decide to plant it in their yards. The touch-me-not is best considered a whimsical houseplant and that's it, unless you find yourself somehow cavorting with cobras—it can be used as a neutralizer for venom. You don't want to mess with how fast it spreads and drops roots, though. Dozens of garden and landscaping message boards are filled with urgent pleas for help on removing the plant before it covers up house pets and lawn furniture like a bad imitation of Miss Havisham's garden from *Great Expectations*.

How I wish I could fold inward and shut down and shake off predators with one touch. What a skill, what a thrill that could be: Touch me not on the dance floor, don't you see my wedding ring? Touch me not in the subway; touch me not on the train, on a plane, in a cab or a limo. Touch me not in a funicular going up the side of a mountain, touch me not on the deck of a cruise ship, touch me not in the green room right before I go onstage, touch me not at the bar while I wait for my to-go order, touch me not at a faculty party, touch me not if you are a visiting writer, touch me not at the post office while I'm waiting to send a letter to my grandmother, let me and my children and everyone's children decide who touches them and who touches them not, touch them not, touch them not.

CACTUS WREN
Campylorhynchus brunneicapillus

In 1986, the tallest saguaro ever recorded—at seventy-eight feet—was blown over by a mighty desert wind in Cave Creek, Arizona. That same year, about thirty miles away, all my friends' front yards featured granite gravel, smooth river rock, and swirls of riprap. Instead of mowing a lawn, we would "rake the rocks" for our chores, and we would sweep them nice and tidy, clean of all little-kid footprints, after an especially sweaty game of *Ghost-in-the-Graveyard*. When our house was newly built and bits of drywall could still be found in the unlandscaped backyard, my parents selected glossy bottle trees, yellow bell shrubs, and Tropicana roses. They never planted a cactus and never wanted to, as far as I could tell—not ocotillo, nor barrel, nor my favorite, the saguaro. And because of this, if I wanted to see a particularly delightful desert bird—the cactus wren—I had to wait until the weekend, when my dad could take us on a hike to the lavender and blush mountains that circle Phoenix. It was always just the three of us, my father, my sister, and me; we had just moved back to Arizona, and my mother was still finishing her contract in Kansas.

What I remember of suburban Phoenix in the eighties: in the Fry's Food and Drug parking lot on Bell Road, an abandoned white roller skate, its neon pink bootlace frayed. I imagine the lace yanked and tugged by a cactus wren, who zooms away with it in her beak—over swimming pool after metallic swimming pool, shimmery as silverfish and headlight—and into her saguaro nest, already decked out with milk caps, tumbleweed, and bits of mossy bramble.

Jason, the kindergartener who lived across the street, had a saguaro two stories tall in his yard, a solid sentinel to stand strong in sunlight and withstand various bored kids throwing rocks. How I wanted a sentinel of my own—to watch out for us if, say, someone in a windowless van followed us home. *That* was the big fear pushed on us in the mid-eighties: the TAKE A BITE OUT OF CRIME slogan from the ubiquitous McGruff the Crime Dog already interrupted our cartoons on every major channel, and could be spotted on billboards along the interstate. *Us* was a whole cul-de-sac of kids who let themselves into their houses because both parents worked. When parents were home, we were hardly ever indoors during the day.

We wore our house keys strung up with yarn around our necks, or fastened with a giant safety pin in our pockets like our moms showed us. Those were the days our teachers told us of kids who never came home from school. The days of *Bridge to Terabithia*, of the fictional girl who went exploring by herself and hit her head and drowned. But not us, we insisted, not us; we'd be too smart to be tricked with candy or the promise of seeing a box full of fluffy puppies. I think fondly now of our school bus groaning to a stop five full and expansive blocks away—farther than I'd ever let my own children walk alone—and of all the latchkey kids who spilled out of that bus, walking the familiar curvy sidewalk back to their empty houses. And bags of potato chips and *Super Friends* or *Scooby-Doo* on the television.

The saguaros stood watch as we walked by with our heavy turtle shell-shaped backpacks. As the oldest of this pack of kids at twelve, I made note of which homes displayed the little triangle-shaped sign in their windows, proclaiming that house was "safe" if anyone ever followed us or tried to get us to come with them into their vehicle. Safety would be ours. We saw the warning commercials every day. We made plans to see each other once our parents came home, because then we would be free to patrol our neighborhood on our bikes. My yard featured no cactus, but rose bushes and yellow bell shrubs dotted the landscape—their pointy seed pods not strong enough to stab someone. Too fragile and crispy. Most of the houses with the yellow signs belonged to retirees. Could they really chase down an unmarked van? We trusted in that yellow. We trusted in the sun and cactus needle.

And we trusted in the cactus wren, in one who knew how to hollow out a space for itself in a most uninhabitable place. When my father would take us hiking up Camelback Mountain, my sister and I could find these birds by just their *chur-chur-churrrr* sounds—a small motor revving up the morning quiet. As birds go, there's nothing particularly showy about them, except maybe their cartoonish white "eyebrow" over their maroon eye. If we were quiet enough, we could watch them perched on a cactus or yucca, scanning the ground beneath for a grasshopper or fallen cactus fruit. The cactus wren, the largest wren in North America at a whopping seven inches long, is one of the only birds that doesn't require standing water to drink—it gets all of its water from juicy insects and fruit.

But perhaps what I love most about these feisty birds is how fierce and crafty they are when they protect their nesting area. The cactus wren's nests are pretty formidable, for the desert; at first glance, it looks as if someone's football has been pricked on a cactus needle, lodged in the armpit of a saguaro. On closer inspection, you'll see a dark hole at one end that leads to a cushy interior chamber. Should you find such a nest, scan the nearby branches, because you'll surely spot another— one of those is a dummy nest, where the male waits to poke and screech at any would-be predators, while the female incubates the eggs safely in the other. Woe to the squirrel or pink coachwhip who thinks they'll be dining on wren egg tonight!

My father worked long hours as a NICU respiratory therapist at Good Samaritan Hospital in downtown Phoenix. I know he must have been utterly exhausted by his week's delicate work and by raising two giggly elementary school-aged girls on his own that year, and yet almost every weekend we headed for the hiking trails of Camelback Mountain. I never saw any other Asian Americans there. I don't know if my father noticed; perhaps he was too busy pointing out mica-edged rocks or ocotillo blooms or the occasional chuckwalla skittering behind a boulder. Or perhaps he was too busy making sure his daughters knew how to tell time with the sun, or how to avoid stepping on wiggly-loose rocks, or how to stay on a solid path. It was one more way we were different from other families in our suburban neighborhood— I didn't know anyone else's dad who took the time to do this with his kids.

As we walked to and from our bus stop—or sometimes to our friends' houses a few blocks away, without our parents really knowing where we were—the saguaros continued to stand guard. Those mighty saguaros gave me a kind of confidence I don't have any more as an adult, confidence that I could stand behind the cactus and not be seen, that my little brown legs could run me around its trunk faster than any man who might approach us, offering candy. Could run me around *any* graveled landscape, leaving small impressions in the rocks for our dads to sweep and rake up on the weekends. Perhaps I wanted to be like the inhabitants of the cacti—those wily birds with a nutty cap of feathers like a brush cut gone awry on their heads, who didn't seem afraid of anything in the harsh and unforgiving desert, no matter their size. We kids of Landis Lane, of Sunburst Elementary in the eighties, knew how to run on desert rocks—how to jump from decorative boulder to decorative boulder to winding bed heavy with smooth river stones—in ways that would send a kidnapper falling. We were tough. Each of us so thin and small boned with spines strong and ready for a fight in case we ever needed to stand and face a shadow lurking over us.

NARWHAL
Monodon monoceros

My sister and I moved from Phoenix to Kansas at the end of fifth grade, this time leaving my father behind, along with a year of jelly sandals and New Coke and trying to catch Madonna on the Live Aid concert. My girlfriends in Arizona and I had Swatches and jelly bracelets stacked up our thin, brown wrists. All the boys I crushed on could break-dance. The only things I knew of Kansas were Dorothy and the Wizard and tornados pointing their creepy fingers all over the state. My mom promised us a giant yard with abundant space to play soccer or throw a football, but I didn't fully understand until we moved how close to her workplace she meant when she talked about the hospital and our home. We lived *on* the grounds of the mental institution, something no kids had done in decades, and the school district had to create a bus stop just for us. When I climbed the school bus steps, I imagined myself a narwhal, with one giant snaggletooth—a saber—to knock into anyone who asked if my sister and I were patients there.

What better animal than the narwhal to blend in with all that Kansan ice, all that white, all that snow? And what better animal to hold its own there? The narwhal is most content swimming in chunky ice, rather than open sea, and can outrace most orca. They hunt formidably despite their cartoonish look and silly nickname, "the unicorns of the sea," as Jules Verne first called them in *Twenty Thousand Leagues under the Sea.*

The narwhal's "horn" is actually a tooth with about 10 million nerve endings—a loooong, helix-spiraled tooth that pokes through the upper left "lip" into the chilly arctic ocean. It's one of only two teeth they'll ever get in their lifetimes. All males have this long-in-the-tooth situation, but about 15 percent of female narwhals also have one, and some narwhals even have a double horn! No orthodontics magic can fix that affair. For a long time scientists thought this tooth was just a hunting tool because narwhals were observed poking smaller fish with it to stun them before gobbling them up, but it's been widely accepted that this tooth also helps narwhals "see" underwater by having have some of the most directed echolocation of any animal. Scientists believe that a narwhal can make up to 1,000 "clicks" per second that can be then transmitted out in narrow or wide rays to search for food or avoid ice. The tusk is also a sensory wand—it is sensitive to salt levels of the ocean and temperature changes, too. The tooth is surrounded by a soft and porous outer layer and filled with a dense inner core packed with delicate nerve endings connected to the brain. Imagine how your teeth would feel after nibbling two or three popsicles in a row, then bowl after bowl of ice cream—imagine a perpetual state of "brain freeze" in your mouth.

Narwhals are found mainly in the Arctic Ocean, but occasionally a small pod of them wanders into a Canadian fjord. The word *narwhal* comes from the old Norse word *nar*, which means "like a corpse," due to the distinctive mottled skin that looks like the spotted skin color of drowned sailors. Narwhals don't have a dorsal fin and they have vertebrae in their neck that allow them to do a whale of a double-take—the only other whales that share these unique traits are beluga. Narwhals eat cuttlefish, cod, and armhook squid. Nothing too disturbing, right? But the *way* they eat can be alarming: a narwhal will swim up to its food very stealthy-like, slow and steady—opening its mouth and inhaling like the world's scariest vacuum—and then, in one giant and powerful gulp, it will swallow the unsuspecting animal whole. Did I mention that narwhals like to swim upside-down? Can you imagine seeing a three thousand-pound narwhal sidling up to you, *upside-down*, and slowly starting to open its mouth?

Who are these toothy creatures' predators? Orcas and the occasional polar bear sometimes hunt baby narwhals. When orcas go after an entire pod, the narwhals just dive, dive, dive—they can survive at almost five thousand feet below sea level. And yet narwhals are classified as "almost threatened," because humans hunt them for their teeth and valuable fat supply.

One afternoon in Kansas, my sister and I were riding the school bus back to the doctor's quarters. As we neared home, I saw my mom in our driveway, unpacking groceries from the car. A chunky blond boy on the bus asked if my mom was Chinese. When I said no, she was actually Filipino, he flipped his eyelids inside out. I cringed and groaned. I can still picture the greasy, dark who-knows-what jammed under his fingernails. Can still see his belly hanging over his Wrangler jeans as he chortled at his own joke. And then, as if flipping his eyelids wasn't enough, he tugged at the skin at the corner of his eyes and pulled it to his ears. *I bet she's Chinese! Her eyes don't even look like yours!*

Ice. Snow. The white plastic of the milk jugs she was carrying in each hand as she smiled at the bus, scanning the faces of all those staring kids for her own. I wanted to dive deep, deep into the darkest of seas so no orcas could find me. I had no sword, and, worse, no sharp tongue with which to sass him back. Instead I just stared straight ahead, gathered up my books, and left without saying good-bye to poor Mr. Johnson, the kindly driver. The narwhal taught me what it was like to see through sound what that boy—someone I would have called my friend until that day—really was.

I could not have known that just one hour south of Larned State Hospital the person I would eventually marry, the father of my sons, was likely practicing layups in his driveway or hitting baseballs into a field not too far from a buffalo range. Just one hour away from my life's love! One hour! A white boy who would one day take my brown hand in his, putting it to his heart when he makes a promise so I can feel his heartbeat and the warmth residing there. If only the narwhal could have taught me how to listen for those clicks of connection, that echo reverberating back to me.

But back then, in sixth grade, all I could see was the dirty snow kicked up in the street by hospital security patrolling for escapees. I know I was quiet that night, and I couldn't figure out why, didn't have the words. It wasn't shame exactly, not anger exactly, but something like a wasp's stinger in the fleshy pad just under my thumb. The pain lingered. Later that spring, a different boy—the smartest, the fastest runner in my class—gave me a ring set with a pink faux zirconia the day after he found out we were moving. *To remember me by*, he said quietly at recess. The gem sparkled, but even then I blanched—I barely liked boys, and I remember thinking it was too much attention, too much shine, too serious.

All I wanted was for him to keep picking me first in kickball teams, have my back if anyone else cracked some racist joke to me again, maybe sit next to me in the cafeteria once in a while—but it was too late, We were going back to Arizona. Still, I had learned there was more to this flat state than a whirl of wind and yellow brick roads. There were good kids here. Kids who, no matter what they learned from television or their own parents, would still reach out for my hand, for a hug, who would miss me on the playground, the way I loved to hang upside-down from the monkey bars with my knees and yelp at the clouds at my feet. I learned that all sunflowers eventually turn toward the sun. Sunflowers so full, my mom would stop her little Chevy Chevette on the side of the road and snap pictures of me and my sister in front of a whole field to send to my dad. *We miss you. We are doing fine in Kansas, but we miss you and will see you soon.* This was our signal, sent across the sea of flowers to my dad, five states away: *We're okay.* Our pod had stuck together. We had made it through the ice and snow and into the spring. Our pod was safe.

AXOLOTL
Ambystoma mexicanum

I f a white girl tries to tell you what your brown skin can and cannot wear for makeup, just remember the smile of an axolotl. The best thing to do in that moment is to just smile and smile, even if your smile is thin. The tighter your smile, the tougher you become.

Give them a salamander smile. The axolotl (pronounced ah-SHOW-lot in Nahuatal, not ax-oh-LOT-ul like I originally thought and first heard) is also known as the "Mexican Walking Fish," but it isn't actually a fish—it's an amphibian. Axolotls are one of the only amphibians that spend their whole life underwater and neotenous, or without going through metamorphosis. Axolotls vary in color, depending on which of their three known chromatophores they inherit—iridiphores (which make axolotl skin shimmer with iridescence), melanophores (shading them a swampy brown), and xanthophores, which turn them a pretty rose gold shade of pink.

Most that are called "wild-type" axolotls have a bright ring around their unblinking eyes like someone took a neon highlighter pen and used it as axolotl eyeliner. Wild-type axolotls have been known to sometimes pop out of their eggs first as the loveliest, ghostly shade of gold with pink eyes, only darkening their skin and eyes as they grow older to blend into their murky surroundings. But for my money, the most striking axolotls are leceustic—pale pink with black eyes. This is the type of axolotl most commonly kept as class pets in hundreds of elementary school classrooms, and it's usually leucistic axolotls—with the pale pink color and that unforgettable upward curve of its formidable mouth that you see—on stickers and t-shirts, and even snuggly stuffed animals.

You remember trying out various shades of Wet n Wild lipstick, including a red the color of candy apples, in the junior high locker room after gym class. Your mother never let you wear lipstick, and boys had not yet begun to notice you. You only wanted to experiment, to hold a tube of color up to your cheek the way you would hold a sequined dress to your body in front of a mirror. Still, you loved the way the lipsticks clacked in your friends' purses like dice, so you decide to try the boldest shade of red. *I don't think someone with your skin tone . . . should wear red. You might want to try this instead,* said the girl who didn't have any brown friends besides you. The only brown folks she knew were on *The Cosby Show.* You adored her, though, and you were the new girl yet again. You didn't want her to stop waiting for you at lunchtime, so you smiled, shrugged, and mumbled, *You're probably right.*

But even from that brief application, you fell in love with and slightly feared that slash of red, a cardinal out

of the corner of your eye, lending definition to the outline of your mouth. A mouth that was used to speaking
only when called upon. A mouth that stayed shut when
you knew the answer because you didn't want anyone to
roll their eyes or mutter *Teacher's pet!* like they had in
years prior. Instead, you wiped off the red lipstick with
wadded-up toilet paper and forced a smile, leaving the
locker room with a pale, cotton candy–colored lipstick
that made you look wan and parched instead.

An axolotl can help you smile as an adult even if someone on your tenure committee puts his palms together as
if in prayer every time he sees you off-campus, and does
a quick, short bow, and calls out, *Namaste!* even though
you've told him several times already that you actually
attend a Methodist church. But it's as if he doesn't hear
you or he does and doesn't care, chuckling to himself
as he shuffles across the icy parking lot, hands jammed
into his pockets. Wide and thin, the axolotl's smile runs
from one end of the amphibian's face to the other, curving at each end ever so gently upward.

Perhaps second in distinctiveness only to the axolotl's
smile are the external gills on stalks that fan across the
back of its head, three on each side, like an extravagant
crown of fuchsia feathers radiating from its neck. The
average axolotl grows to be just over a foot long and
dines on all manner of worms: blood, earth, wax. It also

fancies insect larvae, crustaceans, and even small fish if it can find some.

Scientists have taken to studying axolotls for the regenerative properties of their limbs—very unique in the animal world, because axolotls don't seem to ever develop scar tissue to hide damage from a wound. Axolotls can even rebuild a broken jaw. In recent experiments, scientists have crushed their spinal cords and even *that* regenerates. *Scientific American* reports that you can cut the axolotl's limb off at any point—wrist, elbow, upper arm—and it will make another. One can cut off various parts of arms and legs a hundred times, and *every* time: the smile and a bloom of arm spring forth like a new perennial. Just when one thinks nothing can grow back after such a winter, the tiny, pale shoots of a crocus burst through the sloppy mulch-thin ground after a difficult and heavy sugar snow. An impossible wound begs to differ with its body and says, *I've got another. And another.* These tests involve the repeated amputation of limbs over a hundred times. What does the lab technician say after the ninety-fifth day, perhaps, of this kind of work? *Just five more to go, and we'll close up the report!* How does that person come home and forget those hundreds of estranged arms and legs? It's hard to remember axolotls are endangered when you see their bodies regenerate parts so quickly, when they "smile" at you in aquariums, their pink gills waving as they study you and your own fixed mouth.

Particularly devastating about these amphibians is the fact that the International Union for Conservation of Nature and Natural Resources have determined that there are almost no more axolotls in the wild and have labeled them as "critically endangered." Wild axolotls used to swim in abundance in two particular lakes in Mexico. One of the lakes was drained as a result of the growth of human population—growth in Mexico City— and the other is recently overrun with carp, which gobble up axolotl eggs like M&M's. Axolotls are now found in aquariums and fish supply stores, to be sold as pets.

In spite of the axolotl's seemingly serene visage that often tricks people into thinking of cuteness and perhaps a gentle restraint, axolotls are pretty enthusiastic— sometimes even cannibalistic—in their eating habits. But nature has a way of giving us a heads-up to stand back and admire them at a distance or behind glass— an axolotl's forelegs don't just end with sweet millennial pink stars; they are *claws* designed to help the axolotl eat meat. And when it eats—what a wild mess—when it gathers a tangle of bloodworms into its mouth, you will understand how a galaxy first learns to spin in the dark, and how it begins to grow and grow.

DANCING FROG
Micrixalus adonis

It must be summertime, the season of outdoor dance parties and cookouts, because I just cannot get enough of dancing—and, more specifically, dancing animals. I'm not the only one, either. Recently, the reptile and amphibian world was rocked by the discovery of a record *fourteen* new species of frog. Herpetologists first broke the news in Kerala, the state in southern India where my dad's family is from. This region is a biodiversity hotspot, meaning many of its flora and fauna aren't found anywhere else in the world. All fourteen of the new frogs belong to the genus *Micrixalus*, and herpetologists have named them "dancing frogs."

When I say this, perhaps, you might think of the delightfully named Michigan J. Frog from the old Looney Tunes cartoons. Michigan J. wore a top hat and carried a cane, sang "Hello! Ma Baby," and only danced when people weren't watching. And boy did he ever dance—kicking that leg out with more vim and vigor than any can-can girl. Only male dancing frogs, like Michigan J., exhibit this unusual behavior. The larger the frog, the more frequently they "dance." It's a way of courting and it's also a defensive "stand back, this lady is spoken for" sign, which is needed on the jungle's dance floor,

49

where males often outnumber females a hundred to one. A frog begins by taking his place on top of a wet rock near a cool stream and stretching back one leg at a time. When the leg is fully extended, he spreads his toes as wide as possible, like opening an umbrella, with the webbing between each stretched as far as it can go—a semaphore to tell other male frogs *Go away!* but at the same time says to females, *Hey! Come join the party!*

A dancing frog is about the size of a golf ball and is super sensitive to rainfall patterns and stream levels because of its precise requirements for breeding. After the male and female have met, she begins *her* version of dancing: digging her back feet through pebbles and soil to make a bowl for her eggs. Most often she'll find a spot in a stream where the water just barely covers the rock beds. Too much water, and the dancing frogs might get swept into the current when they try to lay eggs. Too little water, and the eggs won't even touch the stream-bed, meaning almost certain death for her eggs if they dry out completely. After the egg laying is complete, the female shrugs off the mate she's been carrying on her back. He is then free to find another wet rock on which to shimmy and kick the evening away, accompanied by a gurgle of freshwater—a xylophone of accompaniment for this performance.

But alas, the herpetologists' celebrations at their discovery were short-lived. The dancing frogs have already been classified as endangered, due to erratic monsoon patterns in the shola forests of this usually lush and green area of India. Record temperatures have been drying out their habitat, so scientists petitioned the government to protect this relatively small area from deforestation and encroaching pollution. Many herpetologists fear "unnamed extinctions," meaning that more kinds of dancing frogs might become extinct before they've even had a chance to be discovered. And to lose them would be no small disaster—we'd lose their unique connections to eighty-five million years of evolutionary history.

I know that's a sobering thought. But! We have to remember that in a time of so many extinctions, to find fourteen (*fourteen!*) new species of frog is a small ray of hope. Frogs are the great bioindicators of this planet— meaning the health of dancing frogs is indicative of the health of the biosphere itself. That's a bit of promising news to come out of one of the most gorgeous places on earth, where the cool streams flow along the base of the Ghat mountain range in southwestern India. And for now, I'm just so tickled to know these little ones exist, foot-flagging on a shade-cooled rock, tapping their way together toward a rush of pebble, water, wind.

VAMPIRE SQUID
Vampyroteuthis infernalis

Way down deep, in the perpetual electric night of the water column—a place where sunlight doesn't register time or silver filament— the vampire squid glides in search of a meal of marine snow. These lifeless bits of sea dander are actually the decomposing particles of animals who died hundreds of feet above the midnight zone. The vampire squid reaches for this snow with two long ribbons of skin, which are separate from its eight tentacles. If it is truly hungry, it trains its large eye on a glow, the lure of something larger— a gulper eel, perhaps, or an anglerfish waddling through the inky water. The squid's eye is about the size of a shooter marble, but this is nevertheless the largest eye-to-body ratio of any animal on the planet.

If the squid feels threatened or wants to disappear, perhaps no other creature in the ocean knows how to convey that with a more dazzling yet effective show. When the vampire squid pulse-swims away, each of its arm tips glow and wave in different directions, confusing for any predator. To make an even more speedy getaway, the squid uses jet propulsion by flapping its fins down towards its mantel and simultaneously blasting a stream of water from its siphon—all of its arms in one direction. In the next stroke, the squid raises all of its arms over its head in what is called a "pineapple posture." The underside of these arms is lined with tiny toothlike structures called "cirri," giving an appearance of fangs ready to bite down on anything that wants to chase it down for a snack.

As if that wasn't enough to shoo away a predator, the vampire squid discharges a luminescent cloud of mucus instead of ink. The congealed swirl and curlicue of light temporarily baffles the predator, who ends up not knowing where or what to chomp—while the vampire squid wooshes away, meters ahead. It's as if you were chasing someone and they stopped, turned, and tossed a bucketful of large, gooey, green sequins at your face.

I wished I was a vampire squid the most when I was the new girl in high school. We had moved around for so much of my childhood, but the most difficult move I ever made was between my sophomore and junior years. I moved from a class of about one hundred students in western New York to well over five hundred in Beavercreek, a suburb of Dayton, Ohio. I went from sophomore class president to a little no one, a gal who tried out for the tennis team not because I had any interest in the sport but because at practice, at least, I didn't have to be alone. I ate lunch in the library. I ate lunch in a stairwell hardly anyone used. I ate lunch in the dark enclave of the only elevator, hidden outside anyone's eyesight, except for the occasional student on crutches or in a wheelchair. Once I ate lunch—my sad peanut butter and jelly sandwich—while standing up in a scratched and markered-up bathroom stall. To pass the hour, I read the often vulgar, sometimes funny graffiti scrawled on the stall door, just so no one could see that I had no one to talk to.

This was my cephalopod year, the closest I ever came to wanting to disappear or sneak away into the deep sea. I had never feared the first day of classes or meeting new people before. After tennis practice, when everyone else was making plans to meet up at the local pizza parlor, I made myself vanish. I don't know if my teammates even noticed, or wondered where I went.

Oh, I didn't finish high school like that, swimming in darkness. I did end up making friends, giggling with them in the back of the school bus. I joined a bunch of delightfully nerdy pals on the speech and debate team, and I eventually made the varsity tennis team, playing doubles at the district level with my sister. There was no hiding anymore. People noticed when I had to leave parties early for my curfew. They didn't want me to go. And I had a theater / Speech and Debate coach—Ms.

Harding—who wanted me to shine. I know it sounds incredibly precious, but these friends made me believe the mantra, "If one of us does well, we *all* do well." They were generous with their support. Playing it cool was boring. They were my kinfolk, my people—many of whom I'm still friends with today, though we've scattered across the country, spilling out in different directions as fast as we could once we'd tossed our graduation caps in the air.

But there wasn't one specific turning point where I stopped trying to disappear. I don't know how I wiggled out of that solitude, how I made it through the darkest and loneliest year of my youth. No more of those half-eaten lunches hurriedly tossed into the trash. No more make-believe "research" I pretended to do so the librarian would just let me read in peace. Instead, I began scribbling in notebooks and notebooks, trying to write my way into being since I never saw anyone who looked like me in books, movies, or videos. None of this writing was what I would remotely call *poetry*, but I know it had a lyric register. I was teaching myself (and badly copying) metaphor. I was figuring out the delight and pop of music, and the electricity on my tongue when I read out loud. I was at the surface again. I was once more the girl who had begged my parents and principal to let me start school a whole year early. And I was hungry.

I emerged from my cephalopod year, exited my midnight zone. But I'm grateful for my time there. If not for that shadow year, how would I know how to search the faces of my own students? Or to drop everything and check in, really *check*, with each of my sons when they come home from school, to make sure they are having a good time and feel safe? If not for that year where no one talked to me on the school bus, where I had no Valentines, no dates, I wouldn't know what to say to my student with the greasy backpack, who sits in the corner by herself and doesn't make eye contact. Who never talks in her other classes and never spoke in my class unless called upon. I wouldn't know how to tell if her solitude is voluntary or if it covers up a hunger to be seen, to glow with friendship like I had every other year. I secretly love the audacity of her tousled hair, stacked into a giant sloppy bun on top of her head—this student who constantly shuffles in late and is the last to leave but always, always reads ahead on the syllabus. The one who tells me after I come back from being out sick with the flu for a whole week: *I missed you, I am so, so glad you were here today.*

Me too, I say. And I mean it. I wouldn't know how wide and how radiant a student like that could make me smile.

MONSOON

Even when it rains in Kerala, people still ride their colorful scooters, and some even carry a friend or a lover along with them. If a woman is sitting behind the driver, she will ride sidesaddle, wrapped in her sari or churidar. One hand grips the padded rim of the seat for support, the other holds a black umbrella over herself and the driver. The *thwap-thwap-thwap* of raindrops the size of quarters and the scooter's engine are the only sounds worth noticing on their damp course through the village streets.

This rain is never scary, though, even during monsoon. You can tell monsoon is near when you hear a sound in the distance like someone shaking a packet of seeds, then a pause, and then the roar. You know it's coming when the butterflies—fiery skippers and bluebottles—fly in abundance over the cinnamon plants and suddenly vanish. A whole family of peacocks will gather up in a banyan tree, so still, as if posing for a portrait. Then the shaking sound begins.

If you could smell the wind off the wings of an ecstatic, teeny bat—if you could smell banana leaves drooping low and modest into the ruddy soil—if you could inhale clouds whirring so fast across the sky—*that* is what monsoon rain smells like.

Monsoons transform the southwest coast of India into a blaze of fierce verdure twice a year. Of the two rains, the southwest monsoon, between May and August, is the heavier, while the northeast monsoon, in October, is more misty and light, feathering over people's faces from sunrise to dusk—like the mist machines in the produce section of my neighborhood grocery, which inevitably turn on just when I happen to be examining asparagus shoots or a container of juicy raspberries. The southwest monsoon etches metallic rivers such as the Periyar and the Bharathapuzha even deeper and wider, as they flow westward from the rugged Western Ghats, losing themselves in milky conversation in the deep backwaters, and finally depart into the Arabian Sea. At water's edge, coconut trees swoop and tangle low. From a distant bridge, the horizon is nothing but green stars.

Kill a black cobra and hang it in a tree so it will rain.
Rings around the moon mean rain.
Crows can tell of coming rain.
Cows lying down is a sign of rain.
If two doves sit in a frangipani tree, facing the same direction, it will rain.

Swallow four seeds of a violet guava for rain.
Step on an ant and it rains.
Orange moon equals rain.
A dog eats grass? Means rain.

The rain is the constant companion of my grandmother in Kerala, this "land of coconuts." Kerala, land of rain. I am in my first year of graduate school, and although I've visited India previously, my sister and I have never visited without our parents before. Rain murmurs in my ears as I maneuver my way through the markets in Kottayam, the town where my grandmother lives. It trickles down my neck, coalescing into beads on my waxy skin, freshly rubbed with mosquito repellent. In the space between my eyebrows, I am smudged with black: my painstakingly applied liquid bindi drips down the bridge of my nose.

Hot, fat raindrops drench my face even as I stand on our covered back porch. I spy three old women in saris— as graceful as colorful birds scattering at the sight of a mongoose—leaping over the cement wall edged with shards of green bottle glass to steal coconuts from my grandmother's grove. I yell for my grandmother, for her driver, and then shout, *HEY! I SEE YOU!* But it is too late: by the time my grandmother shuffles over in her peach chiffon sari, they have disappeared into the green.

My eleven-year-old cousin Anjana and I sometimes watch MTV India on our grandmother's brown velvet couch. One day, the television sizzles off, thanks to one of the many random power outages in the village. *No Current!* my grandmother calls them. As in, "We must wash the clothes in the morning, before No Current." Or: "You finish the ice cream, or it will waste with No Current." Or: "There are too many babies in this town because of No Current." We sit staring at the screen, two cousins who had only seen each other in pictures until just the week before. Anjana breaks the silence first.

Sometimes, old ladies tie a frog to a ceiling fan. A small frog, yah? And then, they sing out loud that the frog is thirsty and needs water. All the family watches, even the maid. The frog is spinning, spinning from the ceiling, yah? Yuck, yah? Then, then—the next day there is rain!

What happens to the frog? I ask.

Nothing. I think the maid takes it down.

Any squeamishness or misgivings I had about bugs vanished within seventy-two hours of setting foot in Kerala. I've learned the small skitter of insects against the mosquito netting over my bed is loudest when the lights are on, so I make it a point to write aerogrammes to my friends back home only in daylight. Each night, I tuck and retuck the edges of the netting into a tight fit around my cool mattress. I brush my teeth with my right hand, while my left grabs at the air around me, trying to spare my skin from the mosquitoes, already heavy and obvious in the air with someone else's blood. When I open my hand, black asterisks cover my palm.

The next morning, my sister and I beg our grandmother to let the family driver take us to Vembanad Beach, far from the house, damp and silent from the day's power outage. On the half-hour drive there, we pass bare-legged toddlers cupping dragonflies in their hands, faces lit with joy from watching the flutter of blue wings against the gray sky of monsoon. Empty rice sacks are tied together to make roofs for their families' huts. In the early mornings and afternoons, when the rains fall heavy and sure with the scent of bat wing, I wonder how they keep dry.

When the rain stops, terrific smells issue forth—the kind that would make people at a food festival steam and sweat with envy—from curried eggs, thick steaks of broiled fish in coconut milk, chili chicken, payasam noodle puddings, and sweet honey bricks of hulva cooling on wooden tables. Most people here cook outdoors, and neighbors find ways to share their bounty with others less fortunate. Whole households—distant aunts and uncles, maids, drivers, dogs, peacocks, the family cow— lie down for a sweet afternoon nap and wait for the rain to subside so the evening meal can be prepared. Even if the family still feels a bit damp, they are sated and pleased, their bellies full.

How the peacock grew his family: When a naughty boy mistook some oil for a rain puddle, his footprints became greasy little moons. And when those moons clustered and spun into a sugary orbit, they fanned out into a blue breast, and the breast begat milk, and the milk begat a cry—the bird's famous shriek, like someone gargling hot cream and cinnamon.

We arrive at a resort where people can rent houseboats for a day or a week. It's the nearest place that serves ice cream, and it is fortified by generators. A pair of male peacocks stroll near our car and pause in front of us, a little too close—I'm used to birds scattering at the first suggestion of rain or people, but these birds stare straight at us and don't move until my grandmother fans her handbag at them. Kerala's famous coir house- boats wait for the next group of tourists to board before the heavy rains start again. I run to the silty beach, where the Indian Ocean begins a gentle whisk into the

Arabian Sea, while my four-foot-eight-inch-tall grand-mother shuffles the sand, trying to catch up with me. *Aimee, Aimee, you stay here. Ayoo! More bites on your face. What shall I tell your father when I send you home like this? Let's go inside and have your ice cream!*

Cornetto Ice Cream Parlour Menu
Vemby Special Sundaes—49R

THE BOAT— three scoop ice cream, strawberry crush, banana pieces, fruits

ICE CREAM SANDWICH— three slices ice cream, marble cake, caramel nuts, sauce, and jelly

THE APRICOT— vanilla, Spanish delight ice cream, apricot sauce, apricot fruits, almond

THE PASTRY— vanilla and chocolate ice cream, pastry, sauce, caramelised nuts, grated dairy milk chocolate

Vemby Cocktails—39R

VEMBANAD BEAUTY— three flavour ice cream, lychee fruits, marble cake, and black current sauce

MISS GHULBI— gulabjamoon, vanilla ice creams, caramelised nuts, and sauce

CREAM CHANNEL— mix of butterscotch and vanilla ice creams, jelly, crispy nuts, topped butterscotch sauce, and dry fruits

FUNCREAM— vanilla ice cream, jelly, fresh fruits, vermicelli, chikoo, and nuts

PISTAFALOODA— pist syrup, fresh fruits, noodles, jelly, almond nuts, and vanilla scoop

JOKER 2000— it is a funny man for kids with ear, nose, and cap

I choose the Joker because I hardly feel like smiling, with mosquito bites dotting my face, arms, and legs. Last count with a Q-tip and calamine lotion: seventy-five warm lumps. Grandma gives me a quizzical look, like she suddenly smells spoiled milk, but I look away into the swooping coconut trees, trying to be dignified, grown-up, in choosing my dessert. Here the trunks swerve like a wild cursive, palms all full and bursting like green hands spread wide open.

My grandmother is right to doubt me: after the waiter delivers bowls of Miss Ghulbi and Pistafalooda concoctions, he sprints back to our table with my Joker 2000 on a blue saucer so small it could almost be a coaster. My sister looks at me half-sympathetic and half-embarrassed: this is what I summoned the family driver for? It is, of all the things on the sticky laminated menu, the only one that comes premade from some factory in Madras. The supersweet concoction is, true to its description, pathetically shaped into the face of a man with glasses and a baseball cap. Like Mr. Potato Head.

In this village where cold drinks are a novelty (refrigerators are used mainly for meats, and unreliable even then because of the frequent blackouts during monsoon), ice cream is nothing short of luxury. I savor every last cold bite, but I finish before my sister has had two bites of her Miss Ghulbi. I try not to covet her tantalizing bowl of ice cream and sugared nuts, steaming in the humidity. At least I forget about all the mosquito bites swelling on my body, focusing instead on the screeching of peacocks in the distance and the sound of my grandmother's spoon clinking on her bowl, scraping up the last of her pineapple.

Thankfully, my grandmother offers to buy me something else, and suddenly I am eight years old again—quiet and smiling, all traces of my impatience with the heat, the mosquitoes, and the stares of the villagers vanished. I am so grateful. I let her order for me in Malayalam—the language my father uses only when he is angry with me—and I don't even frown when she shares a joke with the waiter where I am obviously the punch line. My sister thinks I receive a Vembanad Beauty, as there are moist vanilla and chocolate cake slices layered with the ice cream, but on the other hand there are no lychee pieces. Instead I find a dark, fruity syrup, like a thinned jam, that blends sweetly with the pure vanilla ice cream on my tongue.

The peacocks continue to trill in the distance. Rain begins to fall. Lean, tanned boatmen steer two-story houseboats along the backwaters with bamboo poles. A small splash of pole—and then quiet. The splash—and quiet. The splash—and quiet. As a houseboat solemnly glides past our table, past our slice of beachfront ice cream parlor, I catch the white flash of teeth from the most dazzling of smiles. I find myself smiling back, and my grandmother watches the whole scene as she scoops the last of her ice cream from her bright aluminum bowl.

CORPSE FLOWER
Amorphophallus titanum

When I was single, the corpse flower was a way to help clear out the sleaze, the unsavory, the unpleasant—the weeds—of the dating world. On a dinner date, when the guy across from me asked something like, *So what are some of your interests?*, I'd tell him about these giant flowers with a seriously foul smell, and how I tracked them down all over the country as they were just about to bloom. Based upon his reaction, I could tell immediately whether there'd be a second date, or if I'd be ghosting him soon.

The corpse flower has the largest inflorescence in the world, with its total height averaging eight to ten feet tall. It only grows in the wild in Indonesia but several botanical gardens in the United States have had much success with growing them indoors. In 1937, the New York Botanical Garden was the first in the country to successfully display one in full bloom.

My own first encounter with a corpse flower occurred at the University of Wisconsin's beautiful campus greenhouse in 2001. I remember being so pleased that the line of people waiting to see the flower was longer than the line to buy Dave Matthews Band tickets in town. It was the heady days of late June, and the greenhouse temperatures were already pushing into the high eighties, but that didn't deter the hundreds who waited for over an hour to get a big whiff of that memorable smell.

This smell is basically what I imagine emanates from the bottom of a used diaper pail left out in the late August sun, after someone has also emptied a tin of sardines and a bottle of blue cheese salad dressing on top and left it there to sit for a day or three. But that smell—and the deep, meaty red of the spathe—is what attracts insects to pollinate the flower before it goes dormant for several years, folding back up into itself.

A few years ago, my husband and I took our boys to the Buffalo Botanical Gardens to see if we could catch a glimpse of "Morty," the corpse flower who was set to bloom any day. As with any outing with two boys under six, the visit ended up taking hours. After the touch-me-not plants, the Venus flytraps, the oversized checkerboard, and the dinosaur topiaries, the boys found the Cactus Room and all of its wild and deliciously dangerous offerings (most of them, of course, eye-level to a child). Before we knew it, the line to see Morty had already wound twice around the lobby. His appearance, after all, drew the biggest crowds in the garden's 115-year history. But the long line was worth it, as my boys' awe—and squeals of disgust—would attest.

The spathe, or the skirt of the corpse flower, is the richest red and maroon. From a distance, its frills look like a plush velvet, an extravagant upside-down winter ball gown. But this "gown" isn't velvet at all; rather it is waxy to the touch. In its center, the chartreuse spadix rises to the sky at recorded heights of over twelve feet. When the two rings of citrus-colored flowers fully bloom and the giant meat-skirt of the inflorescence unfolds, the spadix's temperature approaches that of a healthy human body, one of the only times this happens in the plant world. And the famous smell—oh, the smell—becomes a fragrant invitation to nocturnal insects like carrion beetles.

Some of the names of corpse flowers cultivated in captivity over the last few years, in addition to Buffalo's Morty: Putricia, Wee Stinky, Audrey, Octavia, Rosie, Little Dougie, Terra, Cronus, Metis, Archie, Betty, Clive, Titania, Jesse, 007, Maudine, the Velvet Queen, Maximus, Chanel, Perry, Little John, New Reekie, Aaron, Odie, Ganteng, Sprout, Wally, Morticia, and the Amazing Stinko.

I can't get over the plant's temperature. When you touch the spadix of a corpse flower, it feels almost human, full of blood, and you might expect to feel your hand pulse at its heartbeat. Just last week, I read how trees "speak" to each other underground, how they let out warnings of toxins or deforestation. Trees have also been known to form alliances and "friendships" through fungal networks. All of these findings are still new, but I'm in love with the idea that plants have a temperature, that they can run warm and cold when they need to, that they can send signals to species who will help them, not harm them. And what a magnificent telegraph we might send back, especially if other humans have ever made you feel alone on this earth.

After that first visit in Wisconsin, I spent three years tracking blooming corpse flowers all over the world, and in that time, only one man out of dozens—*one*— didn't blanch at my description of this incredible plant or disparage my enthusiasm. Only one man didn't wince when I said the word *inflorescence*. In fact, this man wanted to know more. He wanted to see a corpse flower for himself. He didn't seem fazed when I reminded him of the odor. I couldn't believe my luck when, a few months later, over what had become our near-weekly dinner date, this handsome, green-eyed man put his fork down and said he wanted to take a road trip with me the next time a corpse flower bloomed. That it didn't matter where it was. I knew he wasn't joking when he said he'd go anywhere with me, and that he meant it. I'd met my match.

Laughing eyes–my mom once observed after she first met him–to describe how his eyes shine at everything, how this man has a knack for making everyone around him feel pretty darn magnificent. *You know, it's very good for a man to have laughing eyes!* But at that moment, his eyes weren't laughing across the restaurant table from me. His serious face told me–through all the electric and fragrant greens, the spray and the shine of the wild bursts of fruit, the messy blood-red days and the stench and the stink too—this finally was a man who'd never flinch, never leave my side when things were messy, or if he was introduced to something new. This was a man who'd be happy when I bloomed.

Seven months later, on the cusp of strawberry season, our friends threw coral-colored rose petals over us as we exited the church, husband and wife.

BONNET MACAQUE
Macaca radiata

The rain in southern India pimpled the lake in the morning and greeted us in the afternoon, smelling of crow feathers and cumin. Our boatmen docked our rented houseboat for the evening in the backwaters of Kerala, and I showed my still-new husband my ankles—the only skin exposed under my broomstick skirt—ringed with mosquito bites. One year prior, dressed in white, I'd walked down the aisle toward this man, and the look he'd given me then is the same he gave me when I asked for the bug salve or told him I needed an aspirin: tenderness.

Shortly after we docked, a honey calf ran out of the jungle, right toward our boat. It took one look at us, shrieked, and stumbled away. I do not have to tell you how frightening it was to see this calf's mama barreling full-speed toward us minutes later, still dragging a piece of fence around her neck, demanding to know what we did with her baby. I thought she would jump onto the deck of our boat and chomp on my thin brown arm. But when she saw our blank looks, she snorted and charged back into the trees.

That was not the end of the surprises. At dusk, we were sitting on the open-air patio of the houseboat when we heard something jump from the coconut trees edging the shoreline to the thatched coir roof of our boat. More thuds followed, each with a small yelp, like a sack of puppies being thrown at the roof. I froze, held my husband's arm, and scanned the shore for any outlines of men among the trees. *What now,* we wondered. We didn't think to call out to the boatmen, who were preparing our curry dinners just fifty feet away, in the cook's quarters. The tiny hairs in my ears pricked awake, trying to place the source of the strange sounds. My husband whispered that everything was okay, it was going to be okay, but I could see his green eyes were open wide and darting.

The sun was almost gone, but suddenly we noticed chips of papaya flesh and vivid chartreuse skins falling from the roof into the bay. Someone or something was eating and making a mess. The plink-plink of fruit pieces and seeds made the water boil with minnows and tiny turtles. The turtles might even be lucky enough to find a defeated dragonfly or wasp.

On the other side of the bay, small fires from distant villages told us where the shoreline began. As the last of the sun disappeared, the fruit showers and thumping stopped. The chattering became higher, more distant. A few moments of silence—then a giant something landed on the roof, and the thatch began to sag with a heavy secret. No more movement. Finally, bravely, my husband poked his head outside and saw the whole scene from the light of the lanterns lit by the boatmen who were already squatting ashore by their own fire and eating their dinners.

Of course! Bonnet macaques were laughing at us from the trees along the shore. The monkeys are common in southern India, and can be found sunning themselves on the rooftops of hotels and tall apartment buildings. They've learned to congregate in parks and near schools, where kids will throw them pieces of plantain or grapes. The fur of bonnet macaques lies somewhere between gray and beige—a true griege—and they stand about twenty inches tall and weigh just over four pounds, a little less than a bag of sugar. The thunk we'd heard was a rather obese wildcat that had chased them away and was now guarding our boat from the roof, refusing to move. It seemed to lie in repose, like Caesar reclining on a chaise lounge, awaiting a snack of grapes. My heart started slamming into my chest. We didn't have phones, and we didn't know the word for "help."

Another boatmen came up out of his quarters to see what the ruckus was about. My friend, you have not known true humility until you've tried to explain to seasoned boatmen that you might be too scared to eat because you think bonnet macaques will attack you. When they finally understood our concerns, the boatmen first looked at each other, then at the bonnet macaques, and finally busted out laughing. Soon Dustin and I were laughing too, and then, to top it off, the macaques started laughing even louder than all of us put together! When the boatmen could finally gather themselves, they advised us that the quiet fat cat still resting on the roof would not harm us, but that we'd better finish our shrimp curry quickly, just to make sure. These cats had been known to boldly lick unattended plates clean.

We finished our delicious meal in a hurry and retreated to our bedroom on the other side of the houseboat. We had never locked the door before, but we locked it that night—as if these macaques would know how to turn a doorknob and latch. From the window I could see the small fires on the other side of the bay slowly extinguished one by one. The scent of plantains hung heavy in the starlit bay.

Bonnet macaques reminded me how good it felt to laugh, to keep laughing in love. To make my love laugh. To let my laughter be from a place of love. The last thing I remember hearing that night was a distant meowing and chatter-like laughter, and I swear, somewhere in the backwaters of Kerala, those bonnet macaques are still having a good laugh over us—a couple trying to navigate that wild jungle, those even wilder early days of this thing called marriage.

CALENDARS POETICA

"**A**rs Poetica" *literally means "the art of poetry,"
and it generally follows that an ars poetica is
thought of as writing about writing—a way of
knowing, of seeing a poet's rhetoric. Here, then, is my
take on writing during the first year I became a mother,
in Western New York:*

June

The white-burst blooms of my clematis whorl themselves into a vine around my mailbox, and each card
and letter I receive has to be pushed through a mouth-
ful of stars. I have just given birth to my first child
over Memorial Day weekend, and so I write exactly *one*
poem this month, but answer each and every card or
letter. My writing instrument is a Sheaffer fountain pen
with a #304 nib. Everything else in my life is chaos: I
am, of course, sleep-deprived, *truly* sleep-deprived, and
the edges of my garden start to blur and shimmer as
if near a gas flame. But when I sit to write, everything
is orderly. I am at the kitchen table. I am away from
the blue glow of my computer. I crave the structure and
formality of handwriting a letter. I select thick sheets of
my favorite peacock-blue stationery, I finger envelopes
lined with thin Japanese block-cut-printed paper, I seal
each correspondence with a round dachshund address

label, and I calligraph each address. My dear husband sets the whole stack of letters into the mouthy mailbox for me. Each afternoon, I watch the mailman when he picks them up, shakes his head at the garish colors of the envelopes, and tucks them into his canvas sack.

July
A blue jay gossips at my window. I nod my head, *Yes, yes. Is that so?*

August
Apple aphids attack my cherry tree, but I am back to some semblance of a writing schedule. We work in shifts, my husband and I. He takes mornings; I am afternoons. I pick blueberries with the baby strapped to my chest, and the lines come to me. Sometimes, if I am lucky, I will remember them when I sit down to write later that day. Mostly, they remain snagged and tangled on the berry branch.

September
My first visiting-writer gig away from my son. Instead of wandering the local sights and shops, I squirrel away in my hotel room in Tempe. Although I do make an appointment with the Frank Hasbrouck Insect Collection at the local college, to see some of its 650,000 insects displayed in steel drawers and glass cases. I read and write at a

superhuman clip. New poems brew and take shape. After I return home, a new school year begins and I make it a point to wear heels after a year of wearing Sensible Shoes. Do the students wonder at my ever-changing belly shape?

October

In my recurring dream, a roc—a monstrous white bird—has carried off Maria, the small elephant I rode last year in southern India, to its nest in the mountains. All the townspeople run out of their homes to look up at the spectacle. Some throw fruit at the roc, trying to save the elephant. I now have the nucleus of my next manuscript set, but each time the dream returns I wake in a light sweat.

November

After a month of readings in Seattle and New York, I am full again. I have two or three small notebooks in my purse at any given time, and it is time to turn the scribbles into stanzas. The last blister beetle, which has vexed me all summer, falls from my dahlias and kicks his leg in a cycling motion. He turns into a midnight-blue shell, crisping in the mulch.

December

If your garden's fruits and vegetables bear thick skin, dimpled and ridged through the fall, it means a severe winter draws near. Cardinals become a gash of red on the page. I write nearly a poem a day this month, each one a small gift to myself. Something for the toe of my stocking. Holly is hung over every door except the one to my office. This office is a riot of pale green and fuchsia, and peppered with images of peacocks, my favorite bird, but I like the door to be plain. I *need* the door plain.

January

The writing is slow but steady. My friends speak of raising chickens once this long winter is over. I wonder about alectryomancy, writing by divination. A white hen is set near a board divided into twenty-six segments. You place grain on each segment, then take down what words are spelled out when the hen eats the grain. On my worst writing days, that's what writing a poem feels like. Only I am not the hen. I am the grain.

February

My son makes his first snow angel, a tiny asterisk in the yard.

March

I hide away in New York's Koreatown for a long weekend, eating spicy noodles and bibimbap. My third poetry manuscript is almost done and it is time to work on my table of contents and the structure of my book. I finish reading three novels in three days. When I get back, I wear my son against my chest around the house and on errands. I need his heartbeat right on top of mine again. I refrain from snipping any of the snowdrops that bloomed while I was gone. I let them stay.

April

Crocus. National Poetry Month: so many readings and events (both given and hosted). Absolutely, positively *no* poems are written this month, although I do sneak in one or two lines while waiting at the dentist. Daffodil. Daffodil. Daffodil. Tulip.

May

I write because the lighter mornings wake me with a dewy promise that there is life after all this ice and snow. I clean my office as a way to procrastinate from writing. Papers from the semester's windy days are sorted and filed. I am shot through with bud and bloom. Strawberry plants have run wild under my porch, and I can smell the pale berries growing in spite of the dark. A nest of cuckoo wasps, the size of a ping-pong ball, grows in the slats of my screen door.

My son takes his first steps—

WHALE SHARK
Rhincodon typus

When the dive master yelled, *Flaaat!* my legs seized with terror and my body tried its best to morph into the shape of a pancake. But since I was floating on the surface of the six-million-gallon Ocean Voyager tank at the Georgia Aquarium, and since my ears were submerged, the command sounded more like *AAABBATTTTTTT!* Just minutes before, we guest snorkelers had been instructed over and over again: *If you hear me shout, "Flat," that means you've got a whale shark swimming directly under you. Flatten your body so your belly doesn't skim her back.* I could hardly believe a fish, longer and wider than a school bus (and weighing more than a fully loaded one!), was swimming directly toward me. I thought for sure I would be swallowed whole by her open mouth.

Improbable, of course—whale sharks only eat plankton and bits of shrimp, and their throats are the size of a quarter—but I could picture it so clearly: my then two-year-old son would never even remember me, would be haunted forever by the loss of his mother, the first known casualty of being accidentally gummed to bits by a gentle whale shark. Such a dumb legacy to leave him in this way! But at the last possible moment before I thought she would crash into me, the whale shark sank just low enough to not touch me at all, though her dorsal fins almost brushed up against the belly of my wetsuit. If I'd wanted to, I could have reached down and petted her spotted back when the dive master wasn't looking, but I was too terrified to do anything but float, lifting my belly and curving my back as far up as it would let me as I tried to get out of the shark's way.

It was as if she was toying with me—wanting to frighten me just enough to let me know exactly who was queen of this tank. The shark repeated her close encounters with me several more times during my snorkel session, even though there were five other snorkelers and two dive masters in the tank. Each time, I watched her giant eyeball, curious as a spaniel's, turn toward my mask. *Very rare to happen at all, let alone to the same person,* said the dive master.

By the time I climbed the metal ladder out of the tank, I could barely walk on the concrete deck. All the muscles in my arms and legs had been tensed for the last half hour, and suddenly even the lightweight snorkel system seemed as heavy as a bag of mulch. In the locker room, I couldn't yet bear to be back into street clothes. When I was sure all the other snorkelers had left to collect their souvenir photos, I sat down on a wooden bench. Still wearing my half-unzipped wetsuit, I wept with my face in my hands.

In my mother's homeland of the Philippines, whale sharks occupy a prominent place in folklore. One of my favorite fairy tales about the whale shark describes the origin of the species, beginning with a greedy teen named Kablay. Kablay lived in a tiny barangay in the province of Donsol, and everyone there knew where he kept his coins. One of his eyes always pointed left, toward the starfruit grove, and the other was always fixed on his coins, in the tin cookie box under his bed. Every night, after his dinner of bangus fish and jelly seaweeds, Kablay pried open the cave-mouth lid of the cookie box. He stacked the coins into a small silver city, then crashed them just to hear the noise. Just to see the light disperse into a hundred pieces on his bedroom floor. Sometimes lizards mistook the dancing light for a flash of moth-wing and crashed into a pile themselves, their whippy tails scattering silver along the floor-boards. Others peered out from behind curtains and shook their heads from side to side, as if to say, *No-no. No-no.* Soon the sound of Kablay counting his money became familiar and expected, a sort of metallic lullaby, in a province that was otherwise quiet, save for the occasional bark of a stray blue-haired dog.

When the Great Typhoon hit and it was clear the dams would not hold, the villagers fled to the hills of Donsol. No time to collect photos, rambutan fruit, or rosaries. Everyone left except Kablay. He sat on the floor in his house and hugged his cookie tin to his chest. The no-no lizards had long since scattered. The waters rushed through the province and swept everything out to sea: tender, young chico trees and whole bamboo stands where at other times you could have bought a sweet fizzy drink poured into a plastic bag with a straw. Even the hapless chickens and stray dogs, mouths wide open, whirled away into the ocean.

But Kablay held tight to his coins and his coins held him. He held them so tight, they pressed into his body and left white spots, one after another, until his whole back was dotted. Kablay's legs shrank into fins, his mouth became a small cave, and the bubbles that popped from it were silver. Sometimes, at sea, you can still see Kablay and his wide eyes searching for a small ship, a scrap of moonlight. And every April he comes back to Donsol to see if he left any coins behind. Kablay's money is always with him, pressed into his dark, leathery skin.And because he loved his coins so much and did not want to part with them, his legs shrank into fins until he turned into a whale shark. The spots on his back look like a whole city of light, where everyone is always awake, trying to remember the simple sweet memory of soil.

Even though I spent almost a year studying whale sharks on my sabbatical, I wasn't prepared for the sheer *size* of one. I wasn't prepared to have a giant hammerhead, a species notorious for sudden attacks on humans, also swimming with me in the tank, watching me with her otherworldly eyeballs spaced so far apart on her wide head. I wasn't prepared for scores of other dangers: blacktip reef, spotted wobbegong, zebra, and sand tiger sharks. *All fed just before we entered the tank,* according to our dive master, *so no need to worry.* Of course I worried.

Looking back at the one and only time I've gone swimming with a whale shark, I realize I was simply unprepared to submit myself so completely to nature. Or rather, humans' interpretation and preservation of nature, by adding 1.8 million pounds of sea salt to a giant tank of water so all these creatures could live and swim together. For science. For entertainment. For spectacle. Perhaps for a little of all three.

I had fulfilled a life's dream, but I couldn't shake my guilt and dread for a long time after. My son could have been motherless. My husband, a widower. And I certainly felt sorry for the sharks. I was able to leave the aquarium and fly home from Atlanta to my family. I was greedy for land, for solid footing again. I knew that whale sharks belong in the wild, where they can do more than trace a slow curve around the same planted coral and faux sea-cliff.

I brought back a whale shark hand puppet for my son. When my family picked me up at the airport, I sat with him in the back seat because I needed to see his sweet pink cheeks again. I reached into my backpack and gave him the present I'd promised him. He promptly slipped it over his tiny fist, which he unclenched to make the puppet's mouth open-close/open-close/open-close. He giggled in his car seat as my husband drove us home. It was as if I had never left them at all.

Almost a decade later, I've visited seas where whale sharks have recently appeared in search of plankton-rich waters, but I've never actually seen one again. *Mommy, Mommy,* my son calls out as he hoists his hand puppet over my shoulder, *I am a whale shark, and I need a snack, please.* He crawls into my lap and talks with the puppet for a bit before he makes the puppet turn back to me and ask, *Where my shark family? Where they?* The whale shark connected to my son contracts, then expands—its furry, pink mouth wide again—and pauses there. In my mind that puppet mouth is still open, waiting for an answer. Perhaps that answer swims in that giant tank, where so many of the beautiful and mighty sharks I once encountered have long since died and have been replaced and replaced and replaced.

POTOO
Nyctibius griseus

In Mississippi, summer means *mosquito*. It also means *tomatoes*, means *mosquito*, means *peaches*, means *humidity*, means *strawberries*, and means *mosquito*. Mostly mosquito. I just counted five while sitting here on my deck, having a coffee at seven-thirty in the morning. What I wouldn't do to have a little potoo bird (or three) in my backyard to catch those bloodthirsty beasties!

Alas, the potoo (pronounced po-TOO) only resides in Central and South America, where it gobbles up said mosquitoes and termites. When fully grown, potoos are a little over a foot tall, with thick necks and giant yellow eyes that look like they've just witnessed a glass-spattered car crash. Their toes and tarsi are a brilliant yellow too, but it's the traffic light eyes that people remember the most.

Some people refer to this bird as little more than a flying mouth and eyes, but potoos are pretty much masters of disguise in the humid jungles of the southern hemisphere. Potoos are nocturnal and so confident of their camouflaging skills that they just sleep right out in the open daylight. They close their giant eyes, tilt their heads toward the tree, and position their cryptic feathers to resemble a broken tree branch that even the sharpest eye struggles to discern what is tree and what is bird. Only a feather-ruffle of wind betrays their otherworldly stillness. Even when they are hungry, they simply wait for insects to fly close and then dart out and return to their home branch with their catch.

Potoos are one of the few birds that never build a nest—males and females take turns warming a single white egg with purple spots settled in a divot of a tree branch. When the baby is born, its feathers are pure white, and when it gets too large to safely hide under a parent, it learns how to freeze *just so* to resemble a patch of white mushrooms.

For a bird famous for its stoic stillness, the potoo's call would sound comical if it didn't sound so scary; if your eyes were closed, you'd never imagine it came from such an austere-looking creature. The call is what you'd get if you combined a tiger roar with a frog croak—if both animals were in severe gastrointestinal distress. If I were in a Brazilian rainforest and heard this cry, I might imagine it was going to be my last day on this planet—that's how chilling and terrifying the potoo cry is. Steven Hilty's book, *Birds of Venezuela,* describes it as "a fairly loud, gruff BUAAaa, descending somewhat . . . like the retching sound of a human." In other words, the stuff of nightmares. Perhaps the reason the potoo leads a motionless, mainly solitary life is to balance its audacious call. There is a time for stillness, but who hasn't also wanted to scream with delight at being outdoors? To simply announce themselves and say, *I'm here, I exist*?

Like the potoo, I grew up wanting to blend in—in my case, with my blonde counterparts—and why would I know anything else? I felt most seen in my childhood not by any television shows or movies but rather when I was in the outdoors, in forests or fields, by lake or ocean. I learned how to be still from watching birds. If I wanted to see them, I had to mimic their stillness, to move slow in a world that wishes us brown girls to be fast. I learned how to call cardinals and have whole conversations with them when I was six. One of the earliest presents I can remember getting from my father is a cardinal-shaped water whistle—if I filled it with water and blew into the plastic straw of its exaggerated tail, I could mimic the distinctive *hurdy-gurdy, hurdy-gurdy* call of the cardinal so well that I could bring cardinals to the edges of our yard, wondering just what I had to say to them.

Eventually I stopped using the whistle and learned how to do it on my own. First in Ohio, while in college and graduate school, when I thought no one might be hanging around the Oval, the main lawn on campus. Second, in Wisconsin, where I lived for a year post-graduate school. During long walks around Lake Mendota, when I'd try to wrestle out a line that vexed me for what would become my first book. Birds have always been an easy audience for me. And I hope I've been an easy, if confusing, audience for them, with my paltry "replies."

These conversations were a secret I kept even from my husband—until one late spring day, when he came home from work early only to find me in the backyard having a lengthy discussion with a riled-up red cardinal and his mate. Both birds, perched just above my head, had seemed to enjoy our talk, but then their metallic chirps sounded more and more insistent, and I have to admit I answered back a little glibly, and then—poof—they burst from the tree and ended our talk right then and there. When I turned around, my husband's mouth was frozen open. Reader, we had been married a decade and this was the *first* time he'd seen me do this.

I'm certain it's not any magic in my mouth, no special twist of tongue that only *I* have unlocked. But I think it's the quiet way you settle into the crook of a tree trunk, the still and slowdown of your heart in a world that wants us to be quick and to move onto the next thing. The secret in talking to birds is in the steadiness of each limb as you make your way into their territory, in the deliberateness of each movement and bend of tree branch and grass blade. And just like the potoo, who is rewarded for her stillness by having her lunch practically fly right to her mouth—perhaps *you* could try a little tranquility, find a little tenderness in your quiet. Who knows what feathered gifts await?

CARA CARA ORANGE
Citrus sinensis

*A*re they ripe yet? This is the question my parents are most often asked since they moved to central Florida. Their neighbors, church friends, and daughters always wonder—it is a guaranteed source of conversation year-round. Within one year of moving from Ohio after my mom retired, my parents were the owners of three navel orange trees, which they had to petition their condo board to plant. And when they built a new house, they dug up and transplanted these three, adding seven more, as well as tangerine and pomelo trees. And just this last visit I found a lemon tree already swollen with fruit, growing as tall as my chin.

Cara cara navels are medium-sized oranges, their skin almost mottled and bruised just from exposure to the elements, and their flesh deep pink, darker than a grapefruit, and so *sweet*. What sets cara caras apart from other oranges, what makes me love them, is their cherry and rose petal smell, the kind you can almost taste after your first juicy bite. And when I visit my parents in central Florida, during winter and spring breaks, that's when the cara cara peaks. In this liminal winter-into-spring time, orange dots weigh heavy in the branches along most highways. You can almost imagine someone is throwing orange confetti as you zoom past in your car. On our long twelve-hour road trips, I look for the glowing orbs along the side of the road in small Floridian towns. There they are: so many cara caras tucked into street curbs after falling out of orange juice factory trucks.

My mother would ask me to eat an orange after breakfast. After lunch. For a snack. For dessert. And I said yes to all of these requests, at first. Until, in the last vestiges of my bratty teenage years, I began to resent the orange. Sometimes I'd say no, just to say no. I wanted to eat an orange of my own volition. My own thought. It pained her when I asked for something different. *Whay another fruit? We hab so many oranges. Your father and I picked them this morning just for you, for you!*

When I got married, I knew she loved my husband, and I also knew she adored my in-laws because she would gift them these oranges, the most precious offerings of her and my father's gardens. After my kids could finally eat solid foods, one of her greatest pleasures was hand-feeding them slices of fresh citrus—all the white threads lovingly pulled off for a sweet bite. Her grandsons would waddle over to her, clap their hands, sometimes even dance a jig in the middle of the kitchen before squawking and chirping for another bit of "onge." *See,* she would tell me, *your sons will be more healthy than you. Look how many slices they want! So tragic you only eat one today!* And then she'd turn back to her little citrus project, and happily mop up their shiny faces glimmered with juice, and laugh at their exuberance, at their jack-o-lantern smiles caused by a new phase of missing teeth.

And now in these slow, winter days in Mississippi—when I ache for the laughter of my parents between semesters—the question of the cara cara comes back to me as I see stacks of other oranges scrubbed clean of any of the natural blemishes found in Florida groves. *Are these ripe yet? Are these? How about this one?* The citrus in the store looks impossible, like the pretend plastic fruit in the plastic basket that came with my sons' toy grocery cart. I have no desire for fruit that bleached over and shiny.

How could I, after the aromatic rose and cherry taste of the cara cara? My sons don't believe me when I say there was ever a time they couldn't pronounce the word "orange". They also can't believe there was a time when they couldn't pronounce the *L* in Florida: *Fo-da! Foda!* When they were small, and I had to sternly remind them it was past their bedtime or forbid them from eating too many cookies, they used to tell me: *No, no—I go to Foda!* Foda—Florida—the place where grandparents let them eat just about anything they could fit in their little bellies. They can't believe, now, that a grocery store might not sell cara caras. *Let's go back to Lola's yard*, my littlest one says as he steers the cart towards the checkout line. *I can pick as many as I want, and she never gets mad!*

Of course she doesn't, I think to myself, as we place groceries on the moving belt. *You and your brother are the very plump and sweet fruit she'd always hoped to one day squeeze.* When daily news seems to bring forth another fresh grief—more children killed, the Amazon rainforest ablaze for weeks—I think of this orange, its sweetness and the smiles it brings to so many families. For the daily tragedies, I try to do what I can to help— donate money, gather bathroom supplies—but my heart longs for a place of tenderness. Where people offer each other, offer strangers, a fresh globe of fruit. *Sure thing, sweetheart,* I tell him as I hoist a melon on the counter. *Let's go back to Foda soon. We are all overdue for a visit.*

OCTOPUS
Octopus vulgaris

A dead octopus turns lavender, like the sky over the Aegean just before the stars appear. The only time I've ever held one in my hands, I was on the island of Thasos, in northern Greece. My family and I were nearing the end of a month-long stay where I spent mornings teaching poetry to students from around the world and afternoons snorkeling with my young sons and husband in turquoise-colored coves. One day, our host at the hotel, Tassos (yes, his name was Tassos of Thasos), announced he'd be hunting octopuses that morning. Right away I asked to join him. I grew especially excited because Tassos was a member of the famed Greek special forces, somewhat akin to the Navy SEALs, and was known around the island for being able to hold his breath underwater for prolonged amounts of time.

Of course we've all heard about the intelligence of an octopus, but probably each of us won't fully grasp just *how* smart and sensitive they are in our lifetimes. Each arm of an octopus forms an asterisk that we might as well apply to any statement we make now about its intelligence. Its brain lies just behind its eyes in what is really the body, not the head—and each time the octopus devours a snack of crab or cockles, the brain can stretch itself if need be to make room for its esophagus. Octopuses are some of the only animals found whooshing and gliding through every single ocean on the planet: Pacific, Atlantic, Indian, Arctic, and Southern. They're known to wheel around anywhere from pelagic ripples near a shoreline to six thousand feet below the surface, huddling close to hydrothermal vents in the deep.

Tassos showed up on the beach at the expected time wearing full snorkel gear and brandishing a speargun. I stayed on the beach with our boys while my husband went into the water with the other faculty and students. The way Dustin tells it, everything people said about Tassos—and more—was true. Tassos could free-dive so deep that the others on the hunt completely lost sight of him—including his shadow—even in the sparkling clear sea.

I collected and jumbled smooth white marble pebbles in my pocket while I waited for their return, their spoils, and tried to find bits of sea glass to cheer up my eldest, whose lip was still quivering from the pain of being left behind. I tried to console him that it'd be too cold, too deep, too scary, but this—this was a mighty injustice, to be left to wander the shore with his mama and little brother, particularly given his love of the hunters' quarry. He had dressed as a cephalopod for Halloween for the previous three years, and most recently as a blue-ringed octopus costume that I stuffed and stitched together for him, complete with eyes made from pop lights.

The horizontal slit of an octopus's eye is a door that judges us. I am certain it knows we humans are messing up entirely, that in just a matter of decades the oceans will become unswimmable to any of us animals. The octopus pupil stays parallel, steady as a raft in calm waters—even if it cartwheels away in a dance—never becoming vertical like a cat's. And the skin around this wondrous eye is marvelous, with the ability to form "lashes" or whiskers spontaneously for protection if it feels threatened. But even if you make an octopus grow lashes, you can be sure its eye will remain fixed on you—you, a creature whose arms have no neural intelligence or taste sensors, not a single one of the *three hundred* suckers that run down the length of each octopus arm. These suckers contains about ten thousand sensory neurons that detect texture, shape, and, most of all, taste. How wild to even have just one sucker on the inside cup of our hands. Just one! For a moment you think the octopus must have something almost like pity for you for your lack.

Once, two researchers at the Seattle Aquarium conducted a test to see if octopuses could tell humans apart.

Each day they more frequently approached their eight resident octopuses, with one scientist holding a bristled stick behind his back, to poke the octopuses with, and the other holding food. The researchers wore the same blue jumpers and were about the same height, and they also changed which side of the tank they approached, but in less than a week, the octopuses could distinguish them correctly. One even aimed its siphon at the researcher with the stick and squirted water at him, and the rest of the octopuses would start moving with something like glee toward the one holding food.

After almost an hour, my husband and the group of ragtag octopus hunters swam back into view. Two of them—my own students—started running toward me and I knew there could be only one reason why. They were cradling an octopus, bringing it back to their teacher, who had been swooning and hoping to see one for most of the month. *Hold out your hands, hurry!* they yelled, and plop-slopped it into my spread fingers. I could see the octopus starting to blanch pale and pulse lavender in my hands, not at all like the healthy mottled violet and nutty beige-red color I had grown accustomed to seeing in aquariums all my life. Its three hearts tapped slower and slower, just minutes away from death, but I didn't know it right away.

Instead I focused on its golden eye, how it fixed upon my shape. How its arms wrapped and drooped around my wrist and up my forearm while it took me in, tasted me. In those moments I held it, how many things it might have felt or known about me. Could it sense the love and exhilaration I felt for it or my sheer despair once I realized it was dying in my hands? I only know that I had never been looked at, consumed, or questioned so carefully by another being.

My eldest started to panic—*Why is it not moving, Mommy? Let's put it back. It's probably so scared!* We tried to revive it in the water, but its lavender body floated in the incoming tide, spectral against the white marble that lined the beach. There had been too much stress, too many hands holding it out of the water; it was all just too much for that creature who prefers solitary senescence, the slow and steady stage of not moving much at all and just taking in the world and water around them. Everyone grew quiet. Some students slipped away to gather up their towels and leave.

My son never ate an octopus again.

GREY COCKATIEL
Nymphicus hollandicus

When Chico, my parents' beloved grey cockatiel, flew away, Dad drove loops around
the lake—windows rolled down in the
ninety-degree heat—calling the bird's name in a thick,
coconutty Indian accent. Mom paced the sidewalks with
Chico's three-story white iron cage hoisted high above
her head, doors wide open in hopes that Chico would
swoop straight home to his ceramic cup of fat sunflower
seeds and bouquet of millet spray.

After my younger sister and I had both settled into
jobs and there was no more threat of either of us needing to move back in with them, my parents did what
thousands of parents do when faced with an empty
nest: they bought a new pet. The grey cockatiel is the
smallest parrot in the cockatoo family. Most of their
body is—you guessed it—grey, but also white, and
most have a creamy yellow face. Cockatiels are famous
for their "cheddar cheeks," tiny wheels of orange on
each cheek, making them the little clowns of the bird
world. They are about three apples tall and slightly
lighter than a deck of cards, living, on average, twenty
to twenty-five years. They are the only parrot whose
tail ends in a point and not a fan-shape. And they are

so easy to take care of—they need at least twelve hours of sleep a day—perfect for retirees.

Every morning, before my parents even had their coffee, my mother would gently remove the blanket over Chico's cage and take the lid halfway off so Chico could climb up and hang out and perch and argue with them until dinner, when he whistled his whistle of I-think-I-want-to-sleep-now. Then my mother would put down her crossword puzzle, close up his cage, say good night to him, and arrange the blanket to darken his cage. It was a good, calm, soothing routine.

But one fateful spring day, after leaving both the garage door *and* the inner door to their house open, my parents quickly found out that neither of them had trimmed Chico's flight feathers in months. A particularly loud motorcycle zoomed down their street, and off he flew, zipping with his fresh freedom down the street and toward the lake.

Cockatiels are the only parrots more famous for their whistling than their talking. Some cockatiels know how to whistle whole tunes, but those are quite rare. You can teach a cockatiel the following tricks: flips, handshakes, how to fly away (and come back) on demand, extending their wings as if they are about to offer up a hug, and whistling on command. Chico knew none of those things, but he did know part of an old folk song in Malayalam: *Tha tha mme poocha poocha! Tha tha mme poocha poocha!* This roughly translates to: *Watch out for that cat!* My parents do not have a cat.

My parents spent all afternoon circling the lake, calling for Chico, to no avail. At twilight Dad wept as he finally pulled into the driveway, and Mom walked to the driver's side window and threw one of Chico's jangly rope toys into my father's lap, hissing, *What's the use, what's the use?*

Surely the hawks or the Florida heat would soon pierce the thin belly of their bird. Dad gripped the wheel tighter, as if trying to catch his heavy sobs into the dark center of his hands, and suddenly, there it was— the shriek they knew so well, the tiny white Mohawk, the splendid flash of yellow and gray—on the tip-top of the persimmon tree. Even the fruit was unharmed by his tender claws. Dad scooped Chico up into the boat of a black umbrella, and my parents cooed over their wild luck. Later that night they clipped the cockatiel's wings in the kitchen sink. My parents slept sound that night after walking miles around their neighborhood lake, their bed made extra soft and so full of hope. As Emily Dickinson once wrote, hope *is* the thing with feathers.

DRAGON FRUIT
Hylocereus undatus

The neon pink of a dragon fruit screams summertime, pop music, sunglasses balanced on the top of my head, weather too warm for socks. It means vintage MTV and stretchy spheres of Bubble Yum popped and snapped in the back rows of a school bus. It's electrocution. It's the shade of lipstick I was never allowed to wear, full of pearl powder and unpronounceable chemicals, the shade worn by Boy George, Whitney Houston, and various members of Duran Duran on the album covers I cherished most.

You would think a fruit that screams this loud would have a veritable pop of flavor, too, but most people agree that the dragon fruit, for all its bluster and noise, tastes like the quietest of melons. Still, the dragon fruits my parents grow in their backyard and proudly bring in a sack when they visit—these fruits hand-watered and tended by my parents—are as sweet as peaches to me. These fruits are native to Central America, but the first time I tried one was at a dinner in Singapore. I was a visiting writer at a university there, and I had brought my mother along as my guest. I was so taken with the color that I went searching for more. During our downtime, I asked a taxi driver to take us to Lau Pa Sat, one of the famous hawker centers full of local food in the heart of Singapore. There, I was assured by my hosts, dragon fruit was a flavor present in many of the food stalls— offered up in colorful shakes and ice creams and jams.

To get to this intensely colored fruit, we begin with one of the most ethereal displays of blossoming I have ever witnessed. The flowers bloom in full for just one evening. That means they have one precious night to be pollinated by a bat or bee, and turn the flower into a dragon fruit. Otherwise the six-inch, greenish-white bloom wilts by sunrise—a whisper of heat and bat wing rattling the crumpled, pale blossom.

Even its name seems like fantasy—including its alternatives: the Cinderella plant, night-blooming Cereus, or simply strawberry pear—but there is nothing fake about the alluring dragon fruit. The bold pink is due to a rind chock-full of lycopene, giving it that scene-stealing shock of color. Each fruit grows to about three to four inches long and is dotted with tender and supple green leaves, like scales on the eponymous dragon. The ghostly white insides carry tiny, black seeds, making it similar in appearance to a kiwi. In fact, its texture and taste are often compared to a muted kiwi—not as sharp, but still sweet—especially when chilled.

There's a lovely cocktail, perfect for the summer, that I like to make on the rare occasion we find dragon fruit in our local supermarket: slice and remove the skin of one dragon fruit and blend the flesh with one-third of a cup of vodka, a dash of freshly squeezed lime juice, and a quarter cup of coconut milk. Toss in a few ice cubes to make the glass sweat. Garnish with an edge of extra dragon fruit for a tropical touch.

On those weeks in Mississippi when the air outside is like a napping dragon's exhalations, there's no sweeter cocktail to lull us out of a sleepy, slow summer evening. If you do catch a sunburn, you can mash up a bit of the dragon fruit flesh and apply it to the tender pink of your skin to help soothe it like an aloe. The dragon can be both the wildness we call out when we see this pink egg, and it can also be the balm. This is the fruit for a time of year when the sun and all its gallop don't merely feel as though they have nudged us from a static winter, but into a fully alive, roaring season—when everything you touch feels like it could give you a blister and a bit of wild burn.

FLAMINGO

Phoenicopterus ruber

A flamingo returns to a soda lake for food and to dance. The dance is legs akimbo, spindle-stick and joint-backward steps from all you know. In hot temperatures, a thick crust of salt is left to bake in the heat—perfect sodium-rich mud to form rock-hard towers, about two feet tall, for nesting its singular egg. Flamingos gather around lakes where few fish can live, so they don't have to compete with anything that eats their favorite food—algae.

My freshman year in college: seventeen and still stretching, my legs outgrew my torso and I shopped for jeans in the men's sections of the thrift stores my friends and I rummaged through after class. Tiny waist and no hips. I didn't yet know this body could break into salt. Boys in their late twenties would cruise us over at UDF (United Dairy Farmers, how Midwestern), the convenience store closest to the freshman honors dorm. My girlfriends and I bought ice cream during study breaks, each of us with a dollar to our names, and we could scrounge up enough to buy a pint to split if we gave a few extra giggles and smiles and promises of parties where we'd be sure to show up later to the checkout guy. But of course these parties were fiction.

To find a monogamous mate to build their egging structure, a flamingo locks step and step with other flamingos, head-flagging with stretches from their mighty
necks and snapping their beaks to the left, then to the
right as they march in unison. The ones who move the
most succeed in finding mates in a dance of mimicry
and rhythm that is marvelous—especially in gather-
ings of upward of several hundred *thousand* birds. It's a
search for the right partner who wants to step together
through one of the longest bird lives on the planet:
about fifty or so years together.

We sometimes danced with these older men at clubs,
and I confess: I was flattered by all the attention lav-
ished on my brown body after years in junior high and
high school being largely ignored by boys those years,
with my pink plastic eyeglasses and nose always in a
book. Since I was twelve, my skinny legs stretching
through the night kept me up and sometimes crying as
I stumbled into my parents' bedroom, moonlight falling
over their bodies. One of them always woke up for me,
shuffled down the stairs to boil water for a hot water
bottle, and massaged my legs until the cries stopped
and I fell asleep with the heat tenderizing my calves.
Tylenol never helped. *You're growing, you're growing,
that's all,* they reassured me the next day. *Your legs will
be so long, and that's good—very good!*

When flamingos sleep, they tuck one leg under their feathers, alternating with their other leg to regulate body heat and keep one leg warm at all times. What we think of as a flamingo knee is actually its *ankle*. A flamingo's actual knee isn't visible through its belly feathers.

I hate to say it looks like marching because that seems to mean war or violence these days, as in a recent case out of Florida. A flamingo named Pinky at Tampa's Busch Gardens was so beloved, she was named the zoo mascot. Pinky became one of the most visited animals at the zoo, with children especially wanting to see the famous bird featured on so many souvenirs inside the zoo's gift shops— until one of the most gruesome zoo animal attacks in Tampa history. People at the zoo that fateful day noticed a forty-five-year-old man acting somewhat erratic, pacing back and forth, but none could imagine why he reached over, grabbed Pinky by the neck—in front of children watching—and hoisted the five-pound bird over his head, throwing Pinky with brute force to the hot cement. Her foot was nearly severed from the trauma. The veterinarians wept as they euthanized her the next day.

My girlfriends and I would hit the college bars for dancing, never drinking anything more than water, and we always walked home in groups or at least pairs. We'd study through the day and maybe take a "disco nap" to help us stay out late. At around nine in the evening we'd start getting ready, and we'd waltz into the bars with barely any ID checks, in boy jeans and chunky black shoes, a mess of choker necklaces, and thin straps of leather bracelets. We'd hear stories of a girl who never made it home. I thought that was just the nineties. Before cellphones to check in and to call for backup from your friends, or to call the police with a few buttons. But twenty-five years later, another story from my alma mater of a young woman missing: *Someone last saw her at a quarter to ten, before the bars even mop and close up.*

We were like flamingos flying long-distance, mostly at night. So many kidnappings happen in the dark, when we think we are safe, in a routine, in a place where "bad things" like that just don't happen. When a flamingo flies in daylight, it does look comical, its long legs dragging down under the fluff of feathered torso.

Someone called the police to say they found her body the next day at a local park.

There is a darkness beneath all dances of color. Everyone associates pink with a flamingo, but a flamingo also has twelve black principal flight feathers, mostly visible when in full flight. Such an unexpected slash under all that fun color.

Someone said she was just finishing up her shift at a local restaurant.

Twenty-five years after my girlfriends and I made dancing from Wednesday to Saturday nights part of our freshman-year routine, I'm now a professor at a big state university. If I'm out late at night, it is usually to pick up something for a late-night craft project for one of my kids. I still look over my shoulder in a dark parking lot. I text my husband to let him know I'm in the car and headed home.

Someone said she was due to graduate in less than three months.

I see young coeds lining the sidewalks near campus on their way to dance. And dance and dance, even in the middle of the week, as I once did. I say a silent prayer for them all to come back safe to their nests late at night, again and again. So far, every one of them has come home. When I see groups of young women out together, I can't help but silently offer something like prayer for them: *Tonight, let them tuck their legs under safe covers, let their parents breathe steady in their own bedrooms and receive no panicked late-night phone calls.*

Under a brilliant moon, and unbeknownst to us, the darkened world silvers and shimmers from pink and ebony wings, a small thunder. We can't possibly hear such an astonishing wind while we try to keep in step with our small dances on this earth. But we should try. We should try.

RIBBON EEL
Rhinomuraena quaesita

When this colorful eel, hidden behind coral, detects a guppy swimming nearby and wants to chase down its next snack, it simply unspools itself, as if a piece of ribbon candy has unfolded and softened in the sea. Or no: that's not right. The wiggle of its body—the undulation to end all undulations—is like my own tongue, excited to tell my husband all the minutiae of a day spent alone with our three-year-old and our infant son, Jasper.

The male ribbon eel's elongated dorsal fin is a screamy chartreuse-yellow and its belly is an attention-grabbing cobalt. The female is entirely yellow and over a meter long. Ribbon eels are all born jet black males—they are protandric, changing to female only when necessary to reproduce. In the span of a month, these females mate, lay eggs, and die, making it exquisitely rare to see even a single female in the wild. The ribbon eel's elongated, leaflike "nostrils," set on each side of its snout, help it detect food scurrying by in the low visibility on the ocean floor. The ribbon eel also has a scruffy yellow goatee on its lower jaw, which stores all its taste buds.

Ribbon eels are mainly content to stay in the same reef hole or coral heap for years, poking their heads out with their mouths ecstatically open as if to say, *Wow—look at this spectacular place I call home!* Really it's just drawing water over its gills to help it breathe, though, and that's how it spends most of its days, most of its brilliant, flat body tucked away. In conditions like these, ribbon eels thrive and live up to twenty years. But the biggest threat to ribbon eels is the home aquarium trade because they don't survive long in captivity. Inside a tank, they soon stop eating, a silent protest against the ugly hands that lifted their elegant bodies up and into a bag or bucket. Most don't last even a year.

If while you are scuba diving a ribbon eel happens to wriggle and flick its way over you, you might not even see it—its underbelly is perfectly camouflaged against the refracted sky above. You might feel a small current as it passes, but when you look up: *nothing.* When I last snorkeled in the South China Sea, I was about three months pregnant and thankful that ribbon eels usually don't linger near the surface. My stomach dropped at the thought of that ribboned muscle, the movement that mimics a cartoon sound wave. I mostly don't fear snakes on land, but seeing that mouth wide open would fill me with a tiny terror, as well as joy, to observe a mouth frozen in surprise and delight at each small fish that swims past.

As a baby, my youngest son was famous among our friends and neighbors for constantly opening his wee mouth in shock and surprise and wonder. He never seemed to be tired. If I turned off a lamp, and whispered that it was time to sleep, and slowly let my eyes adjust to the darkness, I would see him still staring at me with eyes as big as malted milk balls in our moonlit room. His pouty mouth parted in a perpetual state of delight. His wispy eyebrows and fine spread of owl-feather hair. The only time he didn't wear that expression of wonderment was when he blessedly fell asleep, so rare in those early years. But oh—when that finally did happen—how he'd sleep so hard against my chest! We'd both wake in a light sweat, although we were in the middle of a particularly harsh Western New York winter.

And that is how we passed our quiet days at home together during the first cold season of his life, enveloped under blankets while a foot or two of snow fell overnight. Mouths wide open in astonishment at things I'd easily pass over any other time during the busy academic year. I wasn't able to stay home the semester my eldest was born, so I cherished these slow days with my littlest guy, even though that rascal barely slept more than three hours at a time for his *entire. first. two. years.* Maybe the only real thing I could do in those blurry months was marvel. Wonder.

How could I forget the constant clock tick after he'd sat up straight in bed between us, face spotlit by the moon, only getting sleepy again if one of us danced with him in the living room or "toured" the house with him in our arms? I had no language for poems then. I barely had language at all, but I could still exclaim, could still show him all the big and small details of this cave full of simple treasures: *Here is the laundry room, we wash clothes in this machine. This is a closet, I wonder what is inside—oh, a broom and a vacuum! When you are older you get to play with these things and clean the house!* And his favorite: light switches! In every room! The dining room had a dimmer dial, his favorite. I'd save it for last, and he'd kick his footie-covered legs while we slowly approached the dial. But I'd tease him with a quick dash into the kitchen instead: *Look at all these spoons in this drawer! Here's the wedding china we will probably never get to eat off of again! But wait, did we forget this dimmer switch? I wish I knew a baby who knows how to turn this light on! Are YOU that baby?*

Perhaps it is because of these whispered nocturnal adventures during the first years of his life that my son's expressions regularly resemble those of a ribbon eel. Especially here in Mississippi, when our days are mostly spent outside, and it's all: *Mommy! Look at me! Watch this! Mommy, watch me hit a home run! Mommy, did you see that frog?*

Look! Did you see how high I can jump? A hummingbird!
Mommy! When you see a ribbon eel swim, its very expression says, *Look! Look at me! Look at that crunchy shrimp!*

Barring any surprises, this little guy I can still carry on my hip will be our last. Already he is getting too big; I fear this is the last summer I can comfortably carry him around the house. Already he slips out of my arms with such ease. He has finally, finally given up his nocturnal life, and I *almost* miss it. I miss the winding of our bodies around each other, on those rare occasions when we finally *did* close our eyes, tangled in such heavy sleep. He is a jolly child, always moving. Almost every picture I've taken of him since he could walk captures the same expression of pure jubilation in motion. Mouth open wide and calling out to no one in particular. A blur in a red hoodie. Even now he runs from room to room.

He has slipped from my hip, and my husband and I have to constantly remind him to walk and slow down. But thankfully, he still reaches for my hand when we walk through parking lots or cross the street. When we have family movie nights, he grabs a blanket and jumps into my lap and arranges pillows around us: *Look, Mommy! We're in a cave!* He curves his matchstick body against mine so closely I can almost imagine him a toddler again. He has not completely swum away.

QUESTIONS WHILE SEARCHING FOR BIRDS WITH MY HALF-WHITE SONS, AGED SIX AND NINE, NATIONAL AUDUBON BIRD COUNT DAY, OXFORD, MS

If we are going to look for birds all day, is anyone going to be looking for us if we get lost?

I thought you said God has his eye on every sparrow, so why are we counting if He already knows?

Is there a bathroom nearby?

Why won't you let me bring my telescope? There might be birds flying way, way up there, but we can't see them and then we'll mess up The Count.

Why do lady cardinals look so sad and boy cardinals look like they are going to a party?

Someone at school said bees are going missing and if we don't see any more bees, we're going to go missing, too. Is that *true*?

I don't want to be missing. But if I am, can I be missing with you, Mommy?

What about Daddy? I don't want Daddy to be missing.

What is camouflage?

If I wear red and stand behind a cardinal, would you still be able to see the cardinal, or would you only see me?

But isn't that scary for the boy cardinal? He can't camouflage on anything except a red wall.

Or my red shirt. Lady cardinals are lucky! You can hardly see them.

Mommy, you are like a lady cardinal because you are brown.

Why do you have better camouflage than Daddy?

Right now, I have medium camouflage.

Will I be brown or white when I grow up?

Why do some white people not like brown people?

Don't worry, Mommy, you can hide in the forest from those bad people. You have good camouflage.

Can I have good camouflage even though I'm *half and half*?

At school we have to hide under our desks in case of bad people. We did that last week.

It's called "Lockdown"! We have to be quiet like what we're doing now while we wait for birds.

Why are there people who will hunt kids?

If hawks are circling around us, does that mean they think one of us might be good to hunt?

Is there a bathroom nearby?

Why is the redbud tree not called a purplebud tree? All the flowers are purple.

Do hummingbirds ever get tired from flying and just want to swim and float in the water for a while?

Is there anything for them to snack on when they are flying above the ocean, or do they just snack on air and pretend it is a flower?

I think the blue heron is very suspicious. He's so frozen, I feel bad for the frogs and fish that think he is just a bird statue.

If I saw a bunch of turkey vultures looking at the house with their wings out, I would think something scary was going to happen.

Remember when we watched that lady put a tag on a hummingbird?

I bet he didn't like that, and when he got to Mexico, the other birds laughed and asked, *What's wrong with your ankle?* Remember another lady painted a bird on my face at the festival and you made me wash it off at night? I was very sad.

Do birds have eyelids?

Do they ever close them when they fly?

Do they know how to wink at us? Because I think I saw a brown thrasher wink at me last week but I didn't tell anyone.

Is there a bathroom nearby now?

What happens if there is a bird count when I'm forty and we don't find any birds?

Will you be missing when I'm forty?

Will you be missing when I'm *sixty*?

Mommy! What if there were a hundred more green birds in the forest right now, and we just didn't know it? And they were all camouflaged and watching us with our notepads, and we couldn't see them, and they were giggling and telling each other our bird count is all wrong?

Birds don't giggle.

What if they were winking at each other, then?

SUPERB BIRD OF PARADISE
Lophorina superba

O n the day of my wedding, the town square of my sleepy little village in western New York burbled over with a small sea of saris. The town had never seen that many saris and Barong Tagalogs—the men's formalwear of the Philippines, hand-loomed from pineapple fibers—all gathered together before, and our wedding made the front page of the paper. Someone gave us a Barong Tagalog as a wedding present, sized for a tween. *But what if we don't have a child?* I sighed to my husband as we opened gifts. *What if we don't have a son?*

The saris came in every shade. Reds, violets, liquid onyx, and especially teal and turquoise, the colors of the wedding. What a dance party we had at the reception, with these sari colors flashing in the DJ's portable light show. Which is why I was reminded of the *Lophorina superba*—not the lesser nor the greater, but the *superb* bird of paradise—as I looked out at the dance floor.

The superb is a bird of many colors. Its beak is like the blackest-black night in January, when you're trying to write a letter on black construction paper with a black swan feather dipped in India ink: it's pretty black.

When the superb hoists up its long black nape feathers, it looks like it's swooshing an elliptical cape around its neck; it's one of the showiest displays in the entire animal kingdom. Iridescent blue feathers on the superb's head flash extra blue as they catch the sun, little eyes against the black oval of its nape.

This colorful bird dances along at about eight inches tall and lives in New Guinea. It eats mostly fruits and berries but has been known to nosh on the occasional small lizard. The superb bird of paradise leads a pretty solitary life, except during mating season. Perhaps my favorite detail about these birds is that the male actually clears a "dance floor" before he gets his groove on, laying down leaves or scraps of paper to mark the boundaries. Then comes the courtship dance: the bird spreads his black tail feathers in a fan and he starts to jump and bounce before the female while that wide, horizontal turquoise stripe blazes into the shape of a cartoon mouth, the only color emblazoned on those dark feathers.

We had only three songs on the "Do Not Play" list for our wedding DJ: "Strokin'," "The Chicken Dance," and "Macarena." When we were on the party bus on the way to our reception, my new husband received a text from our DJ saying he'd come down with a case of the shingles, but not to worry—he was sending a great replacement and would knock a hundred dollars off our bill.

Unsurprisingly, the dance floor cleared after the playing of four or five songs that no one recognized. People were still smiling, drinking, chatting, but no one was *dancing*. Frantic, I scream-whispered to my husband with my tightest, brightest smile, "Tell. Him. To. Play. ANY. Upbeat. Song. From. 2005!"

Too late: I recognized those rumba notes at once.

But then something extraordinary happened. Not only did everyone take to the floor when "Macarena" blasted over the speakers, but because of its interactive nature, everyone was dancing with each other. My husband's cousin from western Kansas was facing my second uncle from India with outstretched hands. A distant cousin was shaking her hips, wrapped in a pink sari, at one of my best friends from grad school. My husband's grandparents popped their hands behind their heads alongside my dear Filipino friends from New York City, Joseph and Sarah. How did *everyone* know this dance?!

The 1996 music video for "Macarena" is a riot of color: the featured dancers wore silver hot pants, orange headscarves, a pouf of lavender hair, bare midriffs galore, chunky platform shoes. Skin color was a rainbow among the dancers, too—I think it was the first time I had seen an Indian woman in braids and a bindi on MTV. There was a Nordic platinum blonde, an East Asian with a crown of spiky hair-knots, and a gorgeous lead dancer with blond locs. The singers, Antonio Romero Monge and Rafael Ruíz, each wore a dapper black suit. One wore a silver tie, the other copper. They looked as if they were going to a wedding themselves as soon as they were done shooting the video.

I know it's the worst earworm. I know the video is obnoxious with glee. I know the song is now banned from most weddings. But didn't your foot tap ever so slightly when I first mentioned the song? When you first imagined those familiar beats? Wasn't the rhythm just sexy enough to make you crack a slow smile when you first heard those notes? Even a teeny-tiny bit? In one evening, at the beginning of a summer filled with new love and joy, a cacophony of color and laughter and dancing signaled the start of a love story unexpectedly born and grown from the wheat fields of Kansas and the tropical shores of India and the Philippines.

Now, almost fifteen years later, our eldest son—who loves to dance, who has been taking dance lessons since he was three, whose favorite color is also turquoise—will be lanky enough to fit his very own Barong Tagalog when he needs to dress up here in northern Mississippi. What a wonder to have sons who unabashedly love to dance! Who aren't afraid to sway and shake to music whenever they encounter it—and dance to music no one else hears but them. And so, I ask: When is the last time *you* danced like a superb bird of paradise? I mean, when was the last time you *really* cut a rug, and did you mosh, bust a move, cavort, frisk, frolic, skip, prance, romp, gambol, jig, bound, leap, jump, spring, bob, hop, trip, or bounce? Did you dance in the streets? Were you footloose and fancy free? Did you get into a groove, give it a whirl, keep someone on their toes or sweep them off their feet? If it's just you, never fear. It might take two to tango, but it only takes *one* to strut their stuff and shake their tail feathers, even a little bit.

RED-SPOTTED NEWT
Notophthalmus viridescens

I've felt the sting of moving from home to home. But only one move was particularly devastating: moving four hundred miles away after my sophomore year as class president in the tiny town (so tiny it is technically called a village) of Gowanda, New York, to finish out my high school years (and not knowing a soul) in the suburbs of Ohio. My last night in New York was spent with my two fifteen-year-old best friends, Americ and Sara, crying in our sleeping bags through the night, and then over the ruckus of the robins and warblers who greeted us at dawn. We promised to always be in touch and meant it, but at fifteen, when every change seemed ultradramatic, the weight of *this* impending move seemed to shift my whole body into waves of not even knowing how I could possibly live without these girls in my daily life. That morning I rolled up my sleeping bag for the last time with them and hugged my friends good-bye as they drove off to be camp lifeguards at Chautauqua for the summer, and my family headed to our new home in Ohio. Those girls were my first true loves, so much so that The Cure's "Lovesong" was *our* song. I've never forgotten how I swooned listening to that song on repeat in my portable CD player by myself on park benches. How I wrote long, multiple-page letters to them later that autumn—trying to hang on as much as possible to those earlier summer days, but autumn's unmistakable breeze and early chill meant certain wet animals would soon burrow under paving stones or into compost heaps to overwinter.

I look back at the many moves my family made during my childhood and I begin to understand the red-spotted newt more clearly. A red-spotted newt spends years wandering the forest floor before it decides which pond to finally call home. When you spend as long as the red-spotted newt does in a search like this, you grow pickier, more discerning, but are never really salty for long. You measure summers in merry-go-round time, in mental maps of the various walks from your mother's workplace in Kansas to the temporary motel in Iowa you had to live in for a few months, to your dream home you left in Arizona, imagining walks past cactus, riverbed, across neighbors' yards, and past chipped park benches in so many states.

In its juvenile stage, the red-spotted newt—called an "eft"—is a delightful orange with dark red spots outlined in black. These spots warn other animals that if they chomp on the newt, it will be their last meal. These citrus-colored newts carry a similar toxin to the deadly chemicals in a blue-ringed octopus or puffer fish.

Thanks to these spots, fish leave the newts alone; newts are the only type of salamander that can live in harmony with most aquatic creatures. Years later, when the newt reaches its adult stage, all that gorgeous color turns to an olive green, with only the scarcest pops of orange left scattered on its now shiny and glossy wet back.

The newts begin to leave their home pond in their juvenile stage, usually in late summer, after an especially plush amount of warm rain. During walks along park pathways near my home in Gowanda, I could almost always find candy-colored efts at the base of sugar maples if I gently poked at damp leaves with a stick. After exploring dry land for about two to four years, happily thriving in leaf litter or near a particularly muddy stretch in forests east of the Mississippi, most newts almost always know how to come back to their home pond, the very one where they hatched. Scientists in Indiana recently discovered that newts find their way home by aligning with the earth's electromagnetic field. They transported several newts about forty-five kilometers from their home pond and set them up in tanks. Each tank was altered with electromagnets to make the distance feel about two hundred kilometers north or two hundred kilometers south. In every one of the experiments, the newts gathered to the side of the tank, orienting themselves in the direction of their home pond.

These newts are one of the only amphibians to contain a ferromagnetic mineral in their bodies, and that, combined with their incredible capacity to memorize sun- and starlight patterns to return to their original pond waters, make them an animal on par with salmon for their excellent homing capabilities. What's particularly amazing is that in its lifetime—thanks to its innate magnetic compass—a newt usually doesn't stray farther than just over a mile from its original pond, staying within the range of about eighteen football fields.

My own homing instinct was stronger than I ever could have thought. A decade after I left Western New York as a teenager, I was finishing up a fellowship year in Madison, Wisconsin. I scanned the academic job boards for entry-level professorships and had to blink twice when I saw there was an opening not too far from my old home. It was a long shot, I knew, but I applied anyway, even as I drove around to local bookstores and coffeehouses in Madison to apply for jobs there. Coffee barista, English professor—I felt guilty for even daring to hope I could land a tenure-track job—all I knew was that I wanted to stay in the classroom, but I also wanted to be able to spend time outdoors and write.

After a few days' worth of interviews, I received the magical call welcoming me back, and I spent fifteen more years in western New York. I was married there. My babies were born there. But it wasn't my forever home. Though we still keep in touch, my best friends had long since moved away. I was still one of too few brown people in town. I was tired of acquaintances at the post office asking about "my people," meaning Filipinos or Indians; tired of people saying *Namaste!* to me in the grocery store, when I was least prepared for it; tired of the increasingly hostile climate at work if I dared to suggest more diversity on campus; and simply tired of being the one brown friend to so many people. On top of that, I spent fifteen winters navigating roads clogged with lake-effect snow. I was done with that pond. I would need to keep searching.

Sometimes, in the dead of winter—even if a pond has frozen over—you can catch a glimpse of a red-spotted newt skittering under the surface of the ice. Sometimes I wonder what would have happened if I'd spotted such a newt in the hardest, coldest days in New York, when all I could do was daydream of how to move my family anywhere else. I'd like to think if I'd seen those orange-taillight spots, I might have been able to pacify my increasingly restless self, might have been reminded of the promise that no matter how cold your home pond feels, a thaw always draws near, eventually. I'd like to think I would have been reminded to have a little hope and trust that all this time, my immigrant parents had been preparing me to find solace in multiple terrains and hoping to create a feeling of home wherever I needed to be in this country, no matter if people you trust let you down.

I had the tools all along, and I didn't need electricity or a screen to escape. I just needed to change my scenery, my *terrain*. Summer and barbecues and sandals *did* eventually come, after one of the most difficult winters we'd experienced. And later that fall—just like the red-spotted newt—my husband and I felt a pull to come home. This time, though, unlike the newt, we eschewed what was safe, expected, and the only landscape we had ever known as a family, as we were called to a new geography: Mississippi. I could feel a shift in my body the first day we opened the door and stepped foot in Oxford, like tiny magnets in me lined up and snapped to attention because I was *finally* where I needed to be. I could feel it in my bones, my homing instinct pulled me so strongly to this land, a new and exciting landscape for my family to explore—a landscape full of blue sky and whirls of thick kudzu and cricket song.

SOUTHERN CASSOWARY
Casuarius casuarius

The gumball-colored reds and blues of a cassowary's head and featherless neck can make you think of a carnival in the jungle, all festoon and bunting. It's comical from head to toe, really. The black feathers covering its body make the cassowary resemble a dark wig perched on a pair of reptilian legs; its gaze with balloon-y caramel eyes can remind you of a six-year-old's drawing. Each of its curiously plodding footsteps makes it look like it's trying to remember a forgotten dance move. But don't underestimate the cassowary—it is one of the only birds on the planet ever known to kill a human.

Most notably, a Florida man kept a pair of cassowaries as pets. One day in 2019, he tripped as he was checking on the status of a new lime-green egg the female had just laid. The male cassowary startled, leapt on the man, and sliced him to death with its claw. This "murderous nail," as Ernest Thomas Gilliard described it in 1958, "can sever an arm or eviscerate an abdomen with ease," but misguided pet owners aside, usually it's only employed when food is involved. For example, cassowaries can get used to humans feeding them and will begin to approach any human expectantly. If they're denied, they'll kick and slash. Puncture and lacerate. Should this ever happen to you, the last thing you will see on this planet before you bleed out is the rush and wreck of blue skin, and the candy-apple red of the cassowary's wattle swinging like a pendulum above you.

But it's the casque that makes this bird extra distinctive. This hardened, dark growth of keratin on the top of the cassowary's head grows taller with age, eventually stretching a whopping seven inches. The casque helps them figure out the acoustics of their surroundings, amplifying the sounds of a dense forest, helping them run about thirty miles per hour even if there doesn't seem to be a clear path in a forest. Cassowaries run with their heads lowered, so the casque also functions as a helmet. A recent discovery of bones of the *Corythoraptor jacobsi*—a strutting dinosaur that lived during the Late Cretaceous period—revealed a strikingly similar skeleton to the cassowary's, complete with a crest-like casque, reinforcing the cassowary's nickname: *The Living Dinosaur.*

In the world of birds, only the ostrich is taller than the cassowary. Females grow five to six feet tall, taller than their male counterparts, and flash much brighter blue necks. Cassowaries can leap up to seven feet high. They hate dogs and cats and horses, and no one knows why.

They are known to be mostly frugivores, feeding on hundreds of kinds of rainforest fruit, swallowing most whole—but in the wilds of New Guinea and northeast Australia, you can also find them nibbling on myrtle flowers or frogs. Fruit trees benefit from the cassowary's diet, too; scientists have discovered that seeds from the ryparosa, a highly prized Australian tree, are more likely to sprout after a ride through the cassowary's digestive tract. Still, even with the cassowary's natural propensity to help its own environment—*to give back*, so to speak— only 20 percent of their natural habitat remains.

Most cassowary deaths are due to being hit by cars while the birds are scrounging for food too close to a highway. These accidental deaths kept increasing in Australia so its transportation department created special yellow warning signs featuring the distinctive silhouette of the cassowary, a car with a cracked windshield about to launch into the air, and the words "Speeding Has Killed Cassowaries" over a red warning stripe.

In truth, not too many people know about this striking bird. Stores don't carry cuddly stuffed versions for kids to snuggle among their rows and rows of stuffed bears and bunnies. Hardly anyone clamors for a cassowary shirt or a plastic replica in their yard or a shower curtain print, as they do with, say, a flamingo. Cassowaries are hard to keep in zoos; you have to recreate the conditions of a rainforest, provide plenty of space for them to run around, and ideally allow them to swim. Plus they prefer to be solitary. So much space and money to give to just one bird.

But I wonder if it takes a zoo or aquarium for us to feel empathy toward a creature whose habitat is shrinking due to humans, toward a creature most have us have never seen or heard? Their "boom" vocalization registers at the lowest frequency of all known bird calls, mostly below the limits of human hearing. But when they boom to each other in the densest forest, sanctuary keepers report that they can *feel* this rumble in their bones, even if they can't hear it. We usually can't hear cassowaries, but we can literally *feel* their presence, and with their arresting looks, they are one of those ancient birds with a sage look that seem to warn us they won't always be around.

What if the blues and reds of the cassowary's neck could jolt us the same way a traffic light warns us to take care—of ourselves and others—and to obey the rules for driving? The simple fact is this giant and strange and beautiful bird is a "keystone species," meaning the Australian rainforests *depend* on it to maintain biodiversity. And they are dying because of humans.

The phrase "I can feel it in my bones" is synonymous with "I know it to be true." What if the cassowary's famous boom is also nature's way of asking us to take a different kind of notice of them? To not just appreciate and admire cassowaries for their striking looks and deadly feet, but to sense their presence on this earth? Suppose that boom shaking in our body can be a physical reminder that we are all connected—that if the cassowary population decreases, so does the proliferation of fruit trees, and with that, hundreds of animals and insects then become endangered. *Boom*, I want to tell the people at Siesta Key, whom I see dumping empty potato chip bags into the shrubs of sea grapes from my blanket on the beach. *Boom* to the man in the truck in front of me on Highway 6, who tossed a whole empty fast food sack out his window and then, later, a couple of still-lit cigarettes. *Boom*, I want to say to the family who left their empty plastic water bottles on a bench at Niagara Falls State Park, only to have two of them blow over and plummet into the falls. Don't you see? We are all connected. *Boom*.

MONARCH BUTTERFLY
Danaus plexippus

There's a spot over Lake Superior where migrating butterflies veer sharply. No one understood why they made such a quick turn at that specific place until a geologist finally made the connection: a mountain rose out of the water in that exact location thousands of years ago. These butterflies and their offspring can still remember a mass they've never seen, sound waves breaking just so, and fly out of the way. How did they pass on this knowledge of the invisible? Does this message transmit through the song they sing to themselves on their first wild nights, spinning inside a chrysalis? Or in the music kissed down their backs as they crack themselves open to the morning sun? Does milkweed whisper instructions to them as it scatters in the meadow?

Maybe that is the loneliest kind of memory: to be forever altered by an invisible kiss, a reminder of something long gone and crumbled, like that mountain in Lake Superior. Perhaps, in the distant future, a sound that resembles my voice will still haunt my great-great-great-great-great-grandchild—a sound she can't quite place, can't quite name. That sound will prick at her and prick at her. And so will the particular sensation of a sap-sticky pine needle, that chalky kiss, smudging her hands with a pale color found only in the crepuscular hour of the day.

An invisible kiss is like that: the source of what you remember and what stays with you won't come from a single script or scene, but perhaps from a previous haunting or the shock and surprise of remembering the first time you found purple quartz inside a geode. The first time I smashed one by myself, at my son's dinosaur-themed birthday party, I put the rock inside a sock so no shards could slice into the dark iris of my eye. After the first careful taps, I clobbered it, already trying to prepare myself for disappointment: a sock full of dust and crumble. But when I slid out the pieces into my palm, I couldn't believe my luck—out came the tumble and the violet-rich sparkle of amethyst quartz—and suddenly I was transported back to ninth-grade science class. I remembered our timed quizzes to identify minerals on the Mohs scale of hardness. Everyone knew talc was the softest on the scale and of course that diamond was the hardest. Hardly anyone remembered the minerals in between. But *I* was always drawn to quartz. I lingered over it the longest, flipped it over in my hand, even licked it when no one was looking: it tasted like campfire smoke.

A few years ago in our home in Mississippi in the final gasps of summer, a beautiful lime-green chrysalis in the doorway of our front porch that my family had been eagerly watching did not open. My husband and I had never heard of this happening, so we did what we always do when parenthood confounds us: we decided to wait and see. The walls of the chrysalis had grown nearly transparent—our sons could see the familiar pattern of the monarch wing neatly folded up inside. They checked on it first thing when they woke, after racing home from school, and again before bed. My gardening friends said to give it another week. We gave it two. Then three. Still nothing. On more than one occasion I found my youngest squatting down, talking to it, cheering it on, like the monarch was in some kind of race: *C'mon, you can do it! Don't you want to be born, little butterfly? We have lots of milkweed to nibble!*

Butterflies have always been special to my boys. In preschool, my eldest loved them so much, he'd beg me to play videos on YouTube in which butterflies emerge from their chrysalises, and he memorized the stoic narration of their elaborate hatching process verbatim. The one and only time he has ever gotten in trouble at school, in the entirety of his tender twelve years, was when a classmate told him that only *girls* could like butterflies. So he did what any butterfly-loving person would do: he said, *Shut up, stupidface.* Of course, the teacher only heard my son's outburst, which led to the first and only time I marched myself to the principal's office to speak on my son's behalf. But I digress. What I mean is: the monarch butterfly means so much to our whole *family*. Every house we've lived in as a married couple has had plenty of milkweed and other butterfly attractors. In fact, the very first thing we planted in our garden here in Mississippi was scarlet milkweed, a vibrant, leggy plant with a confetti of red-orange blossoms beckoning to butterflies from every tip.

The chrysalis never hatched. One night I heard my youngest include its contents in his evening prayer, but then he never mentioned it again. My husband eventually disposed of it while the boys were at school and neither of them asked where it went, though I know they noticed it was gone. They seemed to understand what my husband and I had known for quite some time: even wings can't guarantee a smooth flight.

BARRELEYE FISH: AN ABECEDARIAN
Macropinna microstoma

About two Eiffel towers deep in the Pacific Ocean, barreleye fish hang almost motionless in the dark, like holiday decorations.

Books, books! Your father tells me you are reading too many books. No more reading at night. No more reading. You want thick glasses like me? No books in the bedroom. You play outside. You don't need books from the book order, that's what a library is for! You want pencil? You want pen? I bring you some pens next time I see you. No more books in bed. Don't read at night! Don't bring books outside. You go play! Why did we buy you a bike?

Contracts for my mom's job back then would last four years or so, which always meant another move right when we started to feel settled. During third through fifth grades, my sister and I lived with my dad in Arizona, while Mom finished out her contract working for a state mental hospital in Kansas. There would be a temporary change when we couldn't take the separation anymore—my sister and I moved to a "Doctor's Duplex" on the grounds of the hospital just to be with her again—but when she had to have a medical procedure done, we landed back in Arizona with only two months left in my sixth-grade year. Boom, just like that, I was back at the school where I already said my goodbyes the year before, walking the wide and airy hallways of Sunburst Elementary.

Deep in the ocean, barreleyes sport a shield around their heads to protect their green, googly eyes. This bulbous shield looks much like the soap-bubble canopy of a helicopter—the glass so wide and round—for great views, say, over and into the Grand Canyon. My mother always scared us about these helicopters, and, when I told her I hoped to ride in one before we left Arizona, made me promise over the phone never to do it. *If you fall out what will I do? Where do you get these ideas of flying? What books are you reading? Why don't you read about something nice, like flowers?*

Eyes of the barrelfish look up, always scanning the dark ocean-night like they're searching the sky for the occasional star, the way I did after a day of roller-skating, in a rink as dark as the sea—save for the dazzle of a mirrored ball in the center. *Don't look down, don't look down,* my friends would yelp to me if I grew dizzy from the spin and whirl of lights at the Great Skate roller rink in Phoenix. Under the mirror ball, the whole rink seemed to move backward although I knew my skates were drifting me forward. *You'll fall if you look down. Eyes up!*

Feeding on jellyfish and the occasional stolen catches from a siphonophore—a skinny invertebrate longer than a blue whale—the barreleye hovers, or station-keeps, at about five inches long. Funny to think of this relatively small fish braving the stinging capsules of the siphonophore's stretchy and lanky-twisty tintella. Above the barreleye's mouth are two dark smudges that were first thought to be eyes, but are actually nares, the fish version of nostrils. Such a tiny mouth puckering in the dark from all the wild smells!

Gosh, how my mom cried when my dad told her I needed glasses. *She reads too much, too much!* I heard her say when I eavesdropped on them from the kitchen phone. *What can I do? She always wants to go to the library!* No matter where we landed during our moves around the country, I always had the library. But carrying my books home proved too unwieldy for my thin brown arms. Once, a librarian spotted us fumbling with our stacks in the parking lot in Phoenix and gave me my first-ever cloth tote bag. I felt so rich: my own book bag! Now I own several dozen and I can't bear to get rid of them.

Head membrane of the barreleye fish forms a transparent dome of skin over its chartreuse eyes. Inside this dome, a barreleye's globular eyes can rotate like binoculars and move to better spy prey directly above them. A clear dome like this acts like a shield to protect the barreleye's eyes from the stinging zap of a jellyfish or a siphonophore. The first planes I ever saw with a dome like that, like those Grand Canyon touring helicopters, were from the top-grossing movie of that year—specifically, on the jets that Maverick and Iceman flew in *Top Gun*.

I ce pops and waxy bags of popcorn handed out in the gym meant it was the last day of school. A group of my fellow bus riders started gathering at the door for the car riders. *Why aren't you in line?* I asked. *We're all going to* _____ *'s house,* my classmate replied. *Her mom is picking us up and taking us to see* Top Gun. *Oh,* I said. *That's right—I forgot that was today. I already had plans. What,* the others wanted to know. *I don't know—but it's big. My dad said it was a big surprise,* I lied. They gave me quizzical looks, and when _____ 's mom pulled up, I watched them giggle into a station wagon, and zoom away.

(J ust so you know, I honestly don't remember the name of that girl who invited every girl in our sixth-grade homeroom to the movies except me. If I could remember, I would definitely name her. Was it you?)

Kicks in the lit-up pool while night swimming made the surface of the water seem like it was boiling over, and I loved those ripples and splashes glowing in the dark, the scent of gyros from our favorite Greek café mixing with creosote from the mountains and faint notes of chlorine. There were no special plans that night, and I simmered about my exclusion that afternoon. These were girls who had been some of my best friends just a year before—but suddenly they were all boy crazy, and I . . . wasn't. But I was eleven. My sister was my best pal, and *she* wanted to float in the pool with me and look up at all the stars. We floated under a radiance of constellations. How could I be salty for long? Maybe my dad would join us and pretend he was a shark or a manta ray. The water was the same color as barreleye fish eyes: electric teal. Once more, I felt so rich because I had my sister, my dad, a now-healthy mom, and a pool to swim in before bedtime.

Loudly some neighborhood kids would sometimes call out, *Google-eyes! Hey, Google-eyes! Where'd you get your goggles?* while I roller-skated at the park. But I could skate faster than any of those kids, and I could pop wheelies with my banana-seat bike. When my circle of friends recreated scenes from *Star Wars* in our cul-de-sac, I always called dibs on playing Darth Vader.

I could be scary if I wanted to. So that quieted their jeers—for a while, at least.

My dad said we could rent *Top Gun* as soon as it came out. Usually it took years for a movie to make it to VHS, but *Top Gun* changed all that. It was the first movie to come out on video the same year it was released in theatres. It was the first blockbuster for Blockbuster, Family Video, *and* Hollywood Video. I remember from the news on TV that the lines for those stores were long and sometimes wrapped through the aisles for a big release. But my dad snagged a copy and waited in line while my sister and I pranced around the store.

Neighborhoods in middle-class suburban Phoenix were full of backyard pools. We learned the impossible art of waiting exactly thirty minutes after meals before diving in. Our pool was small compared to most—not even five feet in the deep end—but it was the only one where I ever heard night-splashing. Our dad seemed to be the only grown-up who let his kids swim under the stars in our cul-de-sac. I have no idea how he had the energy to join us after working long shifts at the hospital. But at night in the pool, the three of us floated on our backs—an unfinished star of our brown bodies without Mom there—and he taught us constellations until we ran out of patience and begged him to play Marco Polo instead.

Of course my father did everything right those years. Though I don't recall having very many toys around, I don't remember wanting for anything or ever being sad for too long, except for sometimes missing my mom at night. I'd say my prayers and think of her when I saw the pink moon through the slats of my bedroom's blinds. During the day, there were endless bike rides and adventures in the neighborhood, and making mixtapes from *Casey Kasem's American Top 40* radio show. A pile of books from the library. Hiking on weekends. Smiles for miles. Of course this isn't true, exactly. But I cannot think of any sustained sadness during that time. Once, he didn't know exactly where to find fluorescent-colored clothing for "Neon Night" at the Great Skate. And another time, he didn't know what I was talking about when I said I wanted more rubber bracelets, like Madonna wore on MTV during those years.

Pink and plastic. My first pair of glasses, and I loved them so much. The whole world sharpened, and I could see cactus wrens and hot-air balloons much more in focus now. My eyes were so good with my pink glasses that I could even see the people in the basket of the balloon waving down at me. And I waved back at them from the center of our cul-de-sac. Eventually the bullies stopped calling me names. One even bought me flowers and snuck them into my desk at school, though my mom made me return them. *Too young! Too young for boyfriends, naman!*

Quite a view while night swimming—in the lit-up pool, skim the floor and rotate till your belly faces the surface and try to hold your breath: When do you start to float up? See the night sky and all its stars from your goggles. In those years, after I started wearing glasses, the sight I missed seeing most with my bare eyes were my Arizona friends while night swimming: the Little Dipper, Draco, Cassiopeia, and the great square of Pegasus, the winged horse.

Running around the back drainage "ditches" behind the new housing developments in our neighborhood meant my pink glasses fogged up, got covered in dust that I'd have to stop and wipe off every so often on my shirt, like I'd seen my father do when he skimmed the pool on weekend mornings. I loved my glasses, but they were a pain for an active kid, and a few years later, when I turned sixteen, I would decide to change to contact lenses instead.

Spookfish are a type of barreleye—the only vertebrates to have mirrors in their eyes. They can see up and down at the same time and follow any flash of bioluminescent light below their body, or even at their side.

Toothless for their vertical gulps, barreleyes depend wholly on shadows and their googly green eyes looking up, down, sideways—all at the same time—when they hunt and slurp and gulp small jellies whole.

Under any sky in the western hemisphere, some thirty years later, no matter what state I'm in—as long as it's a clear night and I'm not near any giant patch of skyscrapers—I can find my old friends. What a gift to spot those bright coins in the sky again.

Various conferences, publishers, schools I've visited—so many tote bags. I keep some in the trunk of my car, some for the farmers' market, and, of course, some for all the books I still check out as a professor and mother to two voracious readers of my own. My husband says we need to donate some, give some away, but I don't want to part with them. An empty bag reminds me of how full I felt just from going to the library. How rich. It reminds me of my four-eyed self, sitting "criss-cross applesauce" (as my boys say now) on the floor of the library until the custodian flicked the lights on and off, as a warning: *Closing time soon, time to make final selections!*

Whole whirls of relief spun like a pinwheel when my mom decided she'd had enough of being away from her daughters. No job was worth it. Even if it meant selling our house in Arizona and our pool. Our entire family was going to move to Gowanda, New York, so we could all live under the same roof finally: in a new, spacious doctor's residence with three large bedrooms. A small park and swing set in front. Rings of maple trees surrounding the hospital grounds. I'd start seventh grade clear on the other side of the country, but again, would be living on the grounds of a mental hospital. I wouldn't see a cactus again for at least another decade.

EXamples of sketches and drawings of the barreleye fish have existed since 1939, but because the transparent, fluid-filled shield disintegrates without the water pressure of the deep, scientists never knew about the membrane until deep-sea cameras were able to catch one in a photo.

Yawning as I picked him up off the couch, up waaaay past his bedtime last week, Jasper, my youngest, said, *Wait, wait—I'm not ready for bed yet. Can I finish one more chapter? Just one more?* All he's ever known about Lola, or *Yaya*, is that she freely grants his wishes. She always lets him read more, lets him stay up later than I would like. Buys him all the books he asks for, and then some.

Zero times has my mother refused my boys' pleas for extended bedtimes, extra ice cream, or more books when she is visiting or when we stay at their house in Florida. Gone are her days of worry and admonitions. In their driveway, my dad now teaches his grandsons how to find constellations, too. The trick to finding constellations is to let your eyes adjust to all that dark. Scientists refer to this as *dark adaptation*. Give them at least thirty minutes to get accustomed to the night sky. If you want to find Pegasus, look for that distinctive square—the plump belly of the horse—look up, look up. The winged horse still flies there without ever losing a feather—over you and me, and all the seas.

DANDELION
Taraxacum officinale

When we were living in upstate New York, I knew that when the last snowmelt ran down the street and the spring peepers began their song, the promise of warmth on my skin was pressing near. *Stars! In the grass!* my son used to say, pointing, when he toddled about our lawn, which my husband and I took as both an indictment and a delight.

As a new homeowner, I obsessed over making our yard dandelion-free. Every dandelion clock, each white blowball about to burst and fly into the wind, was a guilt-inducing sign that I hadn't caught the plants days earlier, when I scoured our yard on my hands and knees, looking to pop them out at the root. What kind of a homemaker would I be if our lawn wasn't trimmed and verdant, no blight spots, and especially no yellow constellations dotting its green?

That toddler is now a tall and lanky teen with a beautiful head of curly-wild hair. We still pick the blowballs ever so carefully, so as not to send the seeds—the achenes—on their pappi, their tiny old man hairs, parachuting across the yard. But I've relaxed a bit about lawn care. Hummingbirds, bees, and monarchs are my priority now. Here in northern Mississippi, I've come to appreciate the extra color in my lawn, knowing my dog and kids can roll and kick around in the grass, pesticide-free.

I can't help but break into a sunny smile when I say the various nicknames for dandelions out loud: *Dogposy. Clockflower. Live-longs. Fortune-teller plant. Bessyclock. Witch gowan. Swine's snout. Tell-time. Lion's tooth. Bumpipe. Heartfever grass.*

And oh, of course, the wishes! So many made since I was a little girl have come true. Hold a dandelion bloom under your chin, and if your skin reflects the yellow, that means your crush is thinking of you. (In other circles, it just means you love butter.)

Best of all—I've come to see so much *deliciousness* to be had from dandelions. There is tea to be made, and wine and coffee, too! Make sure you pluck the kind with tubular stems (not the solid, furry stalks), and soak the blooms in salted water to get rid of any tiny ants lurking. If you find enough yellow florets—four cups of packed petals, to be exact—you can make a jelly that rings a sweetness in your mouth a little like fresh honey. If you can only gather up eighty or so, dip them in egg and flour and fry them in hot oil. Dust them with a touch of paprika and cayenne, and you have yourself a fine, fragrant, crunchy snack.

Dandelions openbloom their faces under the sun and fold like an umbrella at night. My son is far from the only one who called them stars here on Earth. In her poem "A Dandelion for My Mother," Jean Nordhaus writes, "Slowly they turned themselves / into galaxies, domes of ghost stars / barely visible by day." And we are far from the only ones who find them a wonder: "The Dandelion's pallid tube," writes Emily Dickinson, "Astonishes the Grass." How many millions of schoolkids have held up one of those tough green stems to burnish a little yellow on their chins? Have you? We are a year into a global pandemic, and after so much loss, so much of being indoors—I'm looking forward to the return of these starry gifts.

SOUTH PHILIPPINE DWARF KINGFISHER
Ceyx mindanensis

From myths and the crackle-candy of fairy tales, I was taught to fear night. Once, a rain shower shimmered between slats on a roof during the darkest hour and soaked a woman's nightclothes. Two months later, she found out she had a peach growing inside her and was locked in a trunk, dumped into the Aegean Sea. Another time, a woman walks by a pond at twilight and hears a heavy shuffling behind her, so she turns around and the largest swan she's ever seen looks her in the eye and down at her breast and back into her eyes again. No blinking. And then the swan lunges forward and nips at her collarbone.

I want to talk about how it feels to be brown and free in the woods, to not look over your shoulder anymore. To be able to open your hand to a gift. To not listen for footsteps or for someone other than these mucky beauties: Salamander. Squirrel. Mud puddle squelching under your toes. A titmouse jumping from limb to limb. I want to talk about not needing to run anymore, about learning to saunter, even dawdle, in the green.

The brightest color I remember from that first month of the pandemic was violet. Specifically, the violet feathers of the South Philippine dwarf kingfisher. It had evaded scientists for 130 years, but an eye surgeon named Miguel David De Leon was the first person to capture it on film. After ten years of searching, one flew within his sight and, to his surprise, didn't immediately fly away. From beak to tail, the bird is just over four inches, or slightly bigger than a crayon. And you'd need a whole box of them to describe it: Lilac. Lemon-belly. Fuchsia. Rose. Coral with bright blue-violet spots. The most electrically charged array of colors I'd seen in a month of so much darkness and worry and fear.

When I write poetry, I've missed making nocturnes— those observant songs of night—from a real forest, not one from the movies. In Japanese, forest is *shinrin*. Bath is *yoku*. Forest-bathing is *shinrin-yoku*. Names are important. What happened to my heart, the blood sloshing through me and behind my wide eyes, when I was not able to practice shinrin-yoku for years? What quiet violence was that to take away the green light, the pale moonglow, from my brown skin? And from so many other bodies, too?

Once, when I was pregnant with my first child, I was at a retreat in the woods and got lost trying to find my way back to my cabin at night. Thank goodness a pal was driving back to her cottage, saw me stumbling through

the dark, and gave me a lift. I had promised my husband I wouldn't be out late at night, that I'd be careful, but I'd lost track of time and needed the library.
Determined not to get lost the next day, I gathered up
light-colored stones in the bucketfold of my skirt like
Gretel, and placed them into the shape of an arrow
along the trail to the artists' cottages. So by headlamp
or by moon-spell, when I saw the arrow glow and point,
I knew to turn left toward my temporary nest.

The other residents laughed when they saw it, I know.
(I heard.) But they probably hadn't had their wrists
held by two unfamiliar men behind the campus tennis
courts the summer after college. Never had their arms
scratched open from being pinned against a chain-link
fence. Never had to scream with every bit of might from
every alveolus and bronchiole, only to have it all wasted
in the sweaty center of a man's strange palm.

I know the men who laugh long after the women stop.
They laughed at girls with names like mine when they
were boys. They still do. I'm just a chuckle to them. And
I remember every one of those laughs.

Some called me Gretel for the next couple of days: *Gretel,
where's your bike? Gretel, did you save any bread today?*
So be it. Forgive me if I wanted to return safely. Safety

was never given to me. My safety outdoors as a brown girl was never a given.

There are so many birds on this planet found *only* in the forest. So what happens when forests are cut down to make room for another high-rise or resort? We know the answer. But most of us don't want to think about it. What if the South Philippine dwarf kingfisher's colorful plumage was a way of giving us a semaphore, a caution flag, to say, *Haven't you hurt enough? Can you let us keep our homes for once?* Its beak and legs are orange. Its back shimmers the deepest violet, with indigo and coral spots. Its beak looks almost as long as the kingfisher is tall. The proportions can't help but crack me up. You wouldn't think such a small bird would be able to snatch a whole skink and gobble it down, but don't underestimate these little ones—their beaks are formidable in their slicing and dicing.

Thank you, trees. I want to say thank you, thank you, trees—this time to the trees in Mississippi and Kansas for giving me shelter. And now, thank you, to the trees in New Hampshire, for letting me walk under you again at an artist's residency in 2019. For the first time in years, I am glad to be alone in the woods. Some men are like wind—you only notice them when they've done too much or too little—but perhaps one will have the impulse to notice red clover, mockingbird wing, or the small toad at the edge of the pond, instead of leering when a woman carrying a notebook walks past. Someone else can wait for them. Not me. This slow end of summer, I ride a bike and wear a headlamp past midnight on the trails. I haven't been able to do that since I was twenty-one.

The trees give us back ourselves, our tiny cells, the animals and the crocodiles in us. Our fourth crocodile tooth glinting back at everyone who tried to harm us. We are here. We have gifts to give back. To trees who have sheltered trees who have borne witness to all the hurts doled out to brown people. To people with names that jumble and tumble on a tongue. Thank you trees in Mindanao, for providing a home to this bright kingfisher.

South Philippine dwarf kingfishers stay, build, and hunt only in tropical forests, where you can almost feel the water collect behind your knee or in the valleys of your neck. They bop and flit from branch to branch in search of their favorite slippery meal: not fish, but the emerald and coral-bellied skinks that love to hide and sneak in second-growth forests. Habitat loss is this kingfisher's biggest threat.

My name is important. I have been mocked for it all my life. I'll never change it now. I wish more people would care to get tree names right. Teach yourself the difference between red maple and sweet gum. Spicebush and sassafras.

Trees have allowed some bodies to dance this way, that way. They lift their hips, they prance in the forest, unbothered. Some seem to steady themselves. Maybe the floor that they were given is full of pine needles. On one of my nighttime residency walks, I spotted a pair of eyes studying me under the harvest moon. They shone at almost the same level of my own. I fumbled for my weak flashlight. I saw the body, a bright white tail. A tall dog? No—a deer—and two more, behind her.

One hundred and thirty years of avoiding humans trying to capture one in hand or by camera. The last time a South Philippine dwarf kingfisher posed long enough for a sketch, the president of the United States was Benjamin Harrison and Queen Lili'uokalani still reigned in Hawaii. And the one that sat still for De Leon had such a sly look on his face, like he was posing on purpose: *Fine, if you need a little boost of brightness during this global pandemic, take the picture—but hurry up! Hurry up before I change my mind!*

Come sit with me under this water oak. This sugarberry tree. This molave tree. This rainbow eucalyptus. Before I change my mind. Open your mouth and taste the air. Let your mouth be agog, even, and especially, at night. Agape. Agape—which, someone once told me, is the Greek word for the highest, purest form of *love*.

CANDLE LARKSPUR
Delphinium elatum

If you look closely at the tall spikes of the candle larkspur, you'll see a column of buds that resemble dolphins bounding. It's one of the only true-blue flowers out there, with its densely packed neon blossoms and dazzling white centers, called *bees*. Each one wants to leap and splash over the wall in the garden—could they be sending missives from Poseidon, the god of the seas himself? Or are these brilliant royal-blue spikes ridden instead by a goddess of love—Aphrodite—while rosy-cheeked Cupid hangs onto the dolphins' tails as they arrive, ready to bless (or curse!) you with desire?

Candle larkspur can grow up to six feet tall, though my plants have never grown taller than my own five foot four. When I was single, I planted some right outside my home office window in New York, until they spanned the whole window's width. The first things I'd see as I sat down to work in the summer were these pops of blue—blue as the pretend night sky in a planetarium.

A few years later, when I was quiet and pleased with my larkspur and burgeoning garden and life alone, I met Dustin. And a few years after that, candle larkspur were the flowers my friend Sharon and my mother-in-law paired with wheat for mini-bouquets in tin pails and bright blue ribbons, slung over each pew at our wedding—a nod to my husband's Kansas home. Such a pretty sight: lighting the church aisle like an airplane runway, larkspur leading me to the kindest and truest man I've ever known.

I can't grow candle larkspur in Mississippi's blazing hot summers—it's the plant I miss most from my New York garden. But maybe you can. Remember: If you remove the spent flowers through the summer, you'll get another round of blue blooms in the fall. And if you crush these blue blooms and mix them with a bit of alum, you will create the loveliest blue ink. A page of night words to whisper, perhaps, that a garden is in your future? Or perhaps a partner who will write letters to you in the heady days of courtship, and maybe still continues, long after two wily boys are born, each Valentine's Day thereafter?

Or maybe these words will be a candle that lights the way to a totally unknown future yet to unspool and unfurl before you into a gala, a giant party that is your *life*. But for now, in the quiet of birdsong or with the noise of a car honking in the distance—you press and dig on, scraping your trowel. Tapping your hand rake. Wiping your soiled hands on your shirt. Because no matter what, you are *not* alone, not with ten quintillion insects on this planet and 390,900 plants known to science—no, you are most certainly not alone in this rich and dark dirt.

FIREFLY (REDUX)
Photinus pyralis

It is the final week of our stay at the Grisham House, a ten-month residency during the academic year on seventy-seven acres just outside of Oxford, Mississippi. It is highly possible my family will never have this much land all to ourselves ever again, so most of our time is spent outdoors. One of the many reasons my husband and I wanted to stay in this area after the residency was because we could spend more time outdoors in this beautiful town—this "velvet ditch," as the locals lovingly refer to it—in the green and verdant northern part of the state.

One of the biggest treats during this final week at the estate is the abundance of fireflies. With the lights to the estate completely turned off, at first we see nothing—but patience is rewarded when a majestic illumination dots the already humid May air. This past year, under so much wide-open sky and not having to worry about oncoming cars, my sons could fully see the stars without much light pollution for the first time in their young lives. They could pick out constellations readily because, when I lived in Arizona, their grandfather showed me how to do the same. They could identify the Milky Way—the stream of stars—as it poured itself over the estate, and marvel. They don't want to go indoors, ever. They want to stargaze long past their bedtime. My youngest throws his arm around my waist to beg *please*, and when I say yes, they squeal with delight, plunge into the darkness, and race down the driveway and into the field lit only by fireflies. How could I possibly tell them no?

It is this way with wonder: it takes a bit of patience, and it takes putting yourself in the right place at the right time. It requires that we be curious enough to forgo our small distractions in order to find the *world*. When I teach National Poetry Month visits in elementary schools, I sometimes talk about fireflies to conjure up memory and sensory details of the outdoors. Recently, however, seventeen students in a class of twenty-two told me they had never even seen a firefly—they thought I was kidding, simply inventing an insect. So I asked them what they did for fun in that crepuscular-pink time just before dinner. When I was growing up, I played kickball, tag, riding bikes—anything, really, until my parents flicked on the porchlight. But the students' most common answer: video games and movies. In other words, they were always indoors. And usually in front of a screen.

2019 was a banner year for fireflies for much of the Midwest and East Coast. The perfect amount of spring wetness combined with a not-too-severe winter to produce a dazzling display during peak firefly season, mid-June through mid-July. But make no mistake: scientists insist that while a high count of beetles can occur in an outlier year, the overall population of over two thousand varieties continues to *decrease* due to lawn pesticides and light pollution. Because of—and in spite of—this decline in population, artists all over the world seem intent capturing the beauty of these bugs, perhaps as a future reminder of what we once had in abundance.

One of my favorite instances of this tribute is from photographer Tsuneaki Hiramatsu, who shot photos in eight-second exposures of a field where fireflies congregated one summer. He digitally overlapped some of these photos, and the result could easily be mistaken for the night sky on an island in northern Greece or southern India; in Hiramatsu's work, the heavens and earth are lush, luminescent sisters.

It was indeed a sad day when I had to bring up a video online to prove that fireflies do indeed exist and to show what a field of them looks like at night. *Seventeen students of twenty-two had never seen a firefly. Never even heard of them. Never caught one to slide into an empty jam jar, never had one glow in their sweaty hands.* This was in a suburban town where fireflies regularly crowd the edges of less-frequented roads. And it's not just these children. The number of my students who can tell the difference between, say, a maple leaf and an oak leaf has dwindled in my college-level environmental writing classes, too. This shared decrease in knowledge about the outdoors can't be a coincidence.

What is lost when you grow up not knowing the names for different varieties of fireflies? When you don't have these words ready to pop on your tongue: Shadow Ghost, Sidewinder, the Florida Sprite, Mr. Mac, Little Gray, Murky Flash-train, the Texas Tinies, the Single Snappy, the Treetop Flashers, a July Comet, the Tropic Traveler, Christmas Lights, a Slow Blue, a Tiny Lucy, the mischievous Marsh Imp, the Sneaky Elves, and—in a tie for my personal favorite—the Heebie Jeebies and the Wiggle Dancer?

All these names, silent, with still thousands and thousands more small silences following as fireflies hatch, wiggle through their larval stage, pupate, crack out of their shell, and then—winged—decide not to flash their chartreuse light. Scientists *still* don't know how, when, or why fireflies decide to stay visually silent. And even though a field of tall grass might be teeming with fireflies, the space and time *between* flashes have grown longer over the years. There are still wren songs to marvel over. I still need to learn the names of the native insects that will be discovered in the next year alone. And the next after that, and the next.

Where does one start to take care of these living things amid the dire and daily news of climate change, and reports of another animal or plant vanishing from the planet? How can one even imagine us getting back to a place where we know the names of the trees we walk by every single day? A place where "a bird" navigating a dewy meadow is transformed into something more specific, something we can hold onto by feeling its name on our tongues: *brown thrasher*. Or "that big tree": *catalpa*. Maybe what we can do when we feel overwhelmed is to start small. Start with what we have loved as kids and see where that leads us.

For me, what a single firefly can do is this: it can light a memory I thought was long lost in roadsides overrun with Queen Anne's lace and goldenrod, a peach pie cooling in the window of a distant house. It might make me feel like I'm traveling again to a gathering of loved ones dining seaside on a Greek island, listening to cicada song and a light wind rustling the mimosa trees. A single firefly might be the spark that sends us back to our grandmother's backyard to listen for whip-poor-wills; the spark that sends us back to splashing in an ice-cold creek bed, with our jeans rolled up to our knees, until we shudder and gasp, our toes fully wrinkled. In that spark is a slowdown and tenderness. Listen: *Boom*. Can you hear that? The cassowary is still trying to tell us something. *Boom*. Did you see that? A single firefly is, too. Such a tiny light, for such a considerable task. Its luminescence could very well be the spark that reminds us to make a most necessary turn—a shift and a swing and a switch—toward cherishing this magnificent and wondrous planet. *Boom. Boom*. You might think of a heartbeat—your own. A child's. Someone else's. Or some *thing's* heart. And in that slowdown, you might think it's a kind of love. And you'd be right.

ACKNOWLEDGMENTS

Portions of this book appeared as the annual Meridel Le Sueur Essay for *Water~Stone Review*. The essay is meant to honor the writing and contributions of Minnesota writer Meridel Le Sueur, whose work reached out to the larger world via her commitment to social justice.

The buttery kernels of many of these essays first popped in *The Toast*, a website of feminist humor, in 2015 as part of a bimonthly column called "World of Wonder," curated by Roxane Gay and edited by Nicole Chung.

Individual essays or portions of them also appear in the following literary websites and journals:

1966: A Journal of Creative Non-Fiction: "Whale Shark"
Adroit Journal: "Flamingo"
Brevity: "Grey Cockatiel"
The Collagist: "Comb Jelly"
DIAGRAM: "Narwhal"
EcoTheo Review: "Bonnet Macaque" and "Dancing Frog"
Ecotone: "Monsoon" and "Peacock"
Georgia Review: "Cactus Wren" and "Octopus"
Gravy, a journal of the Southern Foodways Alliance: "Dragon Fruit"
Greenpeace.org: "Questions While Searching for

Birds with My Half-White Sons, Aged Six and Nine,
National Audubon Bird Count Day, Oxford, MS"
Guernica: "Monarch Butterfly"
*March Xness: A Yearly Tournament of Essays About
Songs*: "Superb Bird of Paradise"
Mississippi Review: "Potoo"
National Book Critics Circle blog: "Calendars Poetica"
Normal School: "Fireflies"
Orion: "Dandelion"
Oxford American: "Cara Cara Orange"
Paris Review: "Vampire Squid" and "South Philippine
Dwarf Kingfisher"
Shenandoah: "Touch-Me-Not" and "Catalpa"
Stone Canoe: "Calendars Poetica"
Waxwing: "Ribbon Eel"
Terrain: "Corpse Flower"
TriQuarterly: "Southern Cassowary" and "Fireflies,
Redux"

I've said that my books are born of love and wonder, and
I hope what you have in your hands now is perhaps the
most crystalline example yet. So much gratitude to the
following for their support and nourishment:

My barkada, my chosen family: Joseph O. Legaspi, Sarah
Gambito, Oliver de la Paz, Jon Pineda, Patrick Rosal. No one
else I'd rather eat halo-halo (with leche flan!) with than you

all! To Mark Steinwachs, Sharon Wong, Emily VanDette and the entire VanDette family, the Vanwesenbeecks, Jarred Wilson, Deb Knebel, Sara Sutherland, Americ McCullagh, Ron Degenfelder, Christopher Bakken, Allison Wilkins Bakken, Natalie Bakopoulous, and the entire Writing Workshops in Greece program for knowing when to give me quiet and when I needed the sea. For breaking bread with me and for their cheers: the Parsons family, JoAnn DeRosa, Adrian Matejka, Matt de la Peña, the Manganaro family, Meridith Bruce and family, Kaveh Akbar, Paige Lewis, Patrick Phillips, Camille Dungy, Ada Limón, Sean Hill, Lesley Wheeler, and especially Kiese Laymon for lighting a pathway through these essays. To Ross Gay, aka LL Lentils—who read the earliest scratchings of this axolotl. To Beth Ann Fennelly, whose editing pen and tables full of food, drink, and friendship mean the glittery world to me.

I'm especially grateful for Roxane Gay and Nicole Chung for the green light and for shaping these little wonders, giving them their first audience. Special thanks to Laura Blake Peterson and Holly Frederick at Curtis Brown for taking me on. For Rita Dove, Patricia Smith, Jesse Lee Kercheval, Emily Smith, Katrina Vandenberg, the late Brian Doyle, Nick Ripatrazone, Anna Lena Phillips Bell, Jeff Shotts, Matthew Gavin Frank, Leah Wolf, Stephen Church, Ander Monson, Christina Olson,

Elena Passarello, Robin Hemley, Lee Martin, Rigoberto González, Georgia Court, the David Citino family, and Christopher Rhodes, who first shepherded this idea along.

Many thanks and a branch full of creamy magnolia blossoms to my colleagues and students in the University of Mississippi's English department and the College of Liberal Arts; John and Renée Grisham for the space to wonder and wander; the incredible MacDowell Arts Colony, where much of this was revised in the middle of the glorious woods; Kundiman; *SIERRA*; Chautauqua Literary Arts; Hamline University; the team at *Orion* magazine; Copper Canyon Press; Judy Braus and the North American Association for Environmental Education; University of Arizona Poetry Center; University of Nevada-Reno MFA's Distinguished Writer-in-Residence program; the Hermitage Artist Retreat, for time and space to write these essays gulfside; the Georgia Aquarium, Monterey Aquarium, and MOTE Marine Lab; Mississippi Arts Commission for their generous grant; the wonder team at Blue Flower Arts; my favorite bookstore in the world—Square Books—for all their support since I moved to Mississippi; Reverend Doctors Eddie Rester and Chris McAlilly; Fumi Nakamura, for making these plants and animals come to life under her wildly talented hands; and to the entire Milkweed team, especially my publicity powerhouse dynamos—Claire Laine and Joanna R. Demkiewicz—as well as Joey, Mary, Lee, Meagan, Shannon, Allison, Bailey, and Julian. Particular thanks to Daniel Slager, for his vision and enthusiasm (and patience!) from Day One.

Dustin, you believed in this book and my stories first. Your love is the greatest wonder in my life—my writing and whole world expanded when I met you.

Pascal and Jasper—I wrote these love songs to the planet for *you*, to *you*, with *you* in mind. Your golden hearts and laughter and footprints are my most precious wonders.

Mom and Dad—the first poets I ever heard and the greatest storytellers I know—thank you for always taking me to the library and, most of all, for letting me play and wander outside.

An Interview with Aimee Nezhukumatathil
by ROSS GAY

We collaborated on a chapbook of epistolary poems about our gardens called *Lace and Pyrite: Letters From Two Gardens*. I can remember in those poems feeling like, goddamn, it is not easy keeping up! Aimee's images, her beautiful music, her capacity for metaphor: It was a little intimidating. I was definitely learning how to write better poems by being in her company like this. I was also, and more crucially, being schooled in openness, in ardor, in wonder. And I was being schooled in the ways the discipline and practice of wonder deepens my capacity to love what I already love and expands the horizons of what I might. I don't know if I knew it then, but going back to read that chapbook, I see it plain as day. She was showing me a way to make the work that I have come to make.

[. . .] *World of Wonders*, kind of like Aimee, is flabbergasted, gobsmacked, and astonished with glee by all kinds of creatures and phenomena, all kinds of kin, from flamingos to catalpas, from monsoons to corpse flowers, from dancing frogs to axolotls. In addition to being lyrical reveries and love songs and tender remembrances, some of these essays are also alarms, as Aimee writes of the octopus: "I am certain it knows we humans are messing up entirely, that in just a matter of decades the oceans will become unswimmable to any of us animals."

Just before *World of Wonders* was first published back in 2020, we discussed our gardens, family, racism, corpse flowers, singing with birds, teaching, and, of course, wonder.

ROSS GAY: This might be an easy question, or an overly open question, but I am so moved by your study and practice of wonder in this new book, and I kind of just want to ask you if you would talk about wonder for a little bit. Where does it come from for you?

AIMEE NEZHUKUMATATHIL: Thank you so, so much. Wonder for me is when you get surprised by your own curiosity when confronted with something unfamiliar or unexpected and that sense of curiosity turns into a kind of joy and excitement. I moved around a lot as a kid, but the outdoors in any of those places for me was the easiest place of all to exist because I never had to explain myself or my family to anyone. Catalpa trees never asked me, "What *are* you?" So, in summer, for example, I'd be outside as soon as I was done with breakfast, come back inside for lunch, then I'd stay out again till sunset, and sometimes beyond that, to catch fireflies with my friends if I was lucky. If you let yourself be open to wonder, I mean *really* open yourself to being able to receive it, it's the closest thing to falling in love I think—I feel like you can't help but want to protect that animal or plant or person. But, yes, the ethics of wonder raises even more questions, right? Who gets to be outside? Who gets to enjoy being outside? Who gets depicted being outside in books and TV and movies? And if you do have the good fortune of being able to be outdoors for long stretches of time, then I'm guessing you want to tell others about it too—my goodness, how can you not want to share that goodness with others?

GAY: I'm going to keep digging, maybe selfishly, because, as you know, this is in the ballpark of my favorite things to talk about. *World of Wonders* models the practice of trying to be perpetually open to "astonishment" and recognizes astonishment, or wonder(ing), as not only required for transformation, but maybe also required for our survival. Can you talk about that? And the second thing I want to ask you about is the connection between wonder and terror.

NEZHUKUMATATHIL: Oh—yes, that's it! Of course wonder is required for transformation. I mean, without a capacity to wonder about a life—animal or plant—besides your own, how much has been lost? How much violence to the planet and to one another has resulted because of that lack of imagination and wonder? It's staggering. If you can't imagine that cutting down this patch of forest is going to have consequences for house finches, tanagers, towhees, and dickcissels, and *that* in turn will have consequences for insects and moths, and that in turn will have consequences for frogs and snakes and salamanders—well, it's easy to see how this lack of wonder and imagination and care can have terrible generational effects for people, too.

I've been visiting elementary school classes to teach poetry since I was in grad school, and little kids don't have to be reminded or taught to wonder. They naturally are curious and astonished by cloud shapes, leaf shapes—bugs and birds—they have a gabillion questions for me about making a line of poetry, about the planet, and they naturally speak with metaphor. I'll never forget one sweet boy who missed his dead mom and said, "I have a cloud in my pocket," instead of saying *I feel sad.* Something happens, though, in high school or maybe junior high, when some of those same kids are taught that wondering and wandering is silly or uncool, and wanting to learn about the planet and really—about one another—often takes a back seat to what can earn them money. And of course we need money to function, and I love being able to help provide for my family, but I also try to suggest finding a different kind of currency—in addition to, not instead of—another way of being rich: with time, with friends, with knowledge. The Environmental Protection Agency did a study that found the average American spends 93 percent of their time indoors. Ninety-three percent! And this is in spite of so much science that shows how being outdoors is physically and emotionally good for you.

And going back to your question of survival and maybe also terror, too, I think it goes back to if you open yourself to wonder and learn about a plant or animal—human too—that you didn't know about before, like if you knew their names, knew the tender way they took care of their tiny eggs in their very own mouths (jawfish), knew how they used the moon and stars to figure out how to fly home (indigo buntings), knew how they pulled a blanket up to their son's chin on a cold night, I would imagine it would be harder . . . how could you *still* want to make violence on them?

But again I come back to the stark reminder that being outside has long been, and still is, a place of terror for so many. My question for white people—who have long held "power" in deciding who gets to be safe in nature, who gets to decide who or what is represented in nature, and who gets to write about nature in the first place—is: What are you doing, or going to do, to make the outdoors more inclusive and welcoming to others who don't look or move like you?

GAY: Yes, this question recurs throughout *World of Wonders*. In the beautiful essay "Cactus Wren," talking about hiking with your dad, you write, "I never saw any other Asian Americans there. I don't know if my father noticed; perhaps he was too busy pointing out mica-edged rocks or ocotillo blooms or the occasional chuckwalla skittering behind a boulder. Or perhaps he was too busy making sure his daughters knew how to tell time with the sun . . ." You go on: "It was one more way we were different from other families in our suburban neighborhood—I didn't know anyone else's dad who took the time to do this with his kids."

The differences, as you say, are being Asian American in mostly white spaces, and being in love with the outdoors, which are often imagined to be, or constructed as, or preserved as, and policed as, mostly white spaces. That is something that is interesting and moving to me—as someone who loves the woods, a Black man who loves the woods, but mostly doesn't go to the woods here in southern Indiana, with its particular history and present and all these goddamn Dixie flags. I mean, I guess I'm talking about the outdoors as refuge. And I'm talking about your father, this brown dude just in love with and astonished by the earth, and sharing that love and astonishment with you. What was he thinking? What were you thinking? What do you think?

NEZHUKUMATATHIL: You know, I think you are right; at heart this book feels like a love letter to my parents when all is said and done. And also perhaps a long apology and some kind of way for them to know that I was listening and observing, even if it didn't seem like I was interested in what they had to teach me all the time, ha ha. I mean, especially as a teen, the last thing in some ways that I wanted to do was to be on a family vacation to a cave or some remote hiking spot, eating fried rice and cold lumpia on a picnic bench in a state park. But, oh, I can see now that those times were so hard-won and pieced together during their rare breaks from working at the hospital, and they always, always made time for us—it makes me so teary-eyed and just wish so much that I can go back and relish those times with them and my younger sister, you know? What you mention here about the outdoors as refuge to me is so spot-on, though it has taken me several years to fully understand it as such. But from their example in their garden or on vacations, I learned to call back parts of myself that felt unsafe when I was surrounded by so much whiteness—I think we all felt safer outdoors and away from people. I can't say what my dad was thinking, bringing his little girls up a mountain or guiding them through botanical gardens at a snail's pace, but I watched as a little girl how white people reacted to my parents' accents and sometimes spoke to them like children. I never forgot that anger I felt, and I never let anyone treat my parents that way now. But outdoors—no one would challenge my dad's knowledge of astronomy; no one could make a garden bloom better than my mom. I'm sure, I know, my parents feel whole and good outdoors, and I noticed that happiness too.

GAY: Yes, it's such a love letter. You know, I can't read this book without thinking of my own folks, without feeling more grateful to them, really. Could you talk some about how you came to understand your relationships differently as you were writing this book about wonder?

NEZHUKUMATATHIL: One example could be that even though I don't think I ever took my parents for granted, I've come to more fully *understand* what they sacrificed in leaving their families to come to this country and how hard they worked to give me and my sister the life we had, and to figure out ways to do it in spite of not always being welcomed in the country they love so much. When I got married and opened my life fully to my husband, I appreciated my parents' marriage even more, doing so when English was not their first language. And yet they cultivated gardens together as their main common love language, another way for them to communicate. When I became a mother, I appreciated the gift of time they gave me to daydream and catch bugs or spy on robins' nests or climb a tree. And how much they took me to the library in spite of their sometimes seventy-plus-hour workweek; I always had a hot breakfast, and we ate dinners together. My fondest memories of them are all of us outdoors, where they were relaxed and laughing and having meals outside. [. . .]

GAY: It's hard not to ask about the corpse flower, too. I've never seen or smelled one, but now I know. "Corpse Flower" is such a sweet essay—again, the wonder of the natural world allows you to more deeply understand the wonder of a relationship, in this case your emerging relationship with Dustin, who earned your love in part by loving this funky flower. You tell us so many things about the corpse flower—where you first met one, in Madison, Wisconsin; their many names, Morty, Wee Stinkie, New Reekie; even that when they get ready to bloom, they have a temperature about that of a human being. But, as in so many of these essays, you leave me feeling like you could have told me twenty more things—and I want you to tell me a couple of more about the corpse flower, please.

NEZHUKUMATATHIL: Since you asked, it takes about seven to ten years for a corpse flower to finally unfold, and its bulb is only the size of a potato, and I really wish we could have kept the Indonesian name, *bunga bankai*—which is ten times better than what the English called it when they smuggled it out of Sumatra, no? And about four years ago, there was a curious phenomenon—scientists still can't definitively say what was going on—a bunch of *bunga bankai* were suddenly blooming all over the world. At the same time.

GAY: What was going on?

NEZHUKUMATATHIL: Well, the best guess is that several of the corpse flowers now all over the world in botanical gardens are related to one another. Cousins in the plant world, blooming at the same time to help pollinate one another. But no one can quite agree yet on that.

GAY: No, I mean like the poetic answer.

NEZHUKUMATATHIL: Ah, gotcha. Well, then clearly they are all trying to get back to Sumatra. In my book I mention how just before they bloom their temperature gets around ninety-eight degrees—one of the closest plants to human blood heat. And the bloom is them talking to one another, making plans for when they all get to see one another again at home.

GAY: Beautiful. This is your first essay collection, although you've been writing nonfiction for a while and even have your MFA in nonfiction. I'm curious to know how the processes, or maybe more to the point, experiences, of writing these essays were, compared with writing poems. There are things that overlap—exquisite language, precise images, beautiful music, ardor—but the essays are different, and not just because they're longer. So, how was it different?

NEZHUKUMATATHIL: Honestly, I started getting more frustrated with the tyranny of the line break in poems. For me writing nature and doing extra research for each essay felt like an unspooling or unfurling of language that I didn't want interrupted with a line break's tension. And I also was interested in a kind of rising action and denouement from building sentences—as opposed to lines—that I don't ever think about when drafting a poem. I almost always start my poems with a very specific image, and I start my essays with a very specific scene in mind. When the writing of an essay is going good, I mean really taking off—it feels like clean laundry strung up in the summer sun. It feels free and like the snap-snap of a sheet in the wind, the words in a solid sentence click-snap into place. The writer Brian Doyle said, "The world is still stuffed with astonishments beyond our wildest imagining—isn't that the most alluring sentence ever? Isn't that the sentence we should have pinned up on every bathroom mirror in the world, so we all see it first thing in the morning every blessed day before we brush our excellent choppers?" I don't have this taped up on a mirror, but I do have this written inside of my writing notebook.

GAY: [. . .] It seems like *World of Wonders* comes from a [. . .] cultivated field of practices: attention, play, openness, tenderness, love.

NEZHUKUMATATHIL: Absolutely. But it's informed by my very distinct experiences as a mom, wife, daughter, friend, etc. And being a woman with brown skin in this country. I'm reminded how growing up I never saw anyone who remotely looked like me outdoors. If there was an Asian person in a book or on a screen, they were dead serious, or the villain, or the computer nerd, or an actual "gong" sound effect rang out when they had any actual dialogue. Tired tropes. Such a lack of imagination from those writers, isn't it? I honestly cannot ever recall seeing an Asian American even smile once in any television show or movie or music video. And I certainly never saw an Asian depicted *outdoors*. Imagine going your whole childhood and never seeing anyone who looked like you *smile*? Look around us— just about every hurt we see in the news is caused by a person's lack of imagination, a lack of curiosity about their fellow human beings, a lack of wonder. How could

I *not* want to set the groundwork for my sons so they grow to be curious adults who let themselves be filled with awe, unapologetically. How could I not wish to celebrate and cultivate wonder now?

Adapted from "World of Wonders: An Interview with Aimee Nezhukumatathil" by Ross Gay, published in the September/October 2020 issue of Poets & Writers *magazine.*

Wonder Prompts

MAKE A SKY JOURNAL! Designate any blank notebook your Sky Journal—nothing fancy, a spiral notebook will do. This is low-stakes writing. Even if you can't make a full poem or essay, you can designate a notebook into just having a place for your observations about the sky. (1) Record day/time of your observation of the moon. (2) Make note of what phase it is in. Don't know all the phases? Look them up—draw and label them in your notebook. (3) Make a cloud report! Note the day/time. (4) Describe and/or sketch the clouds. (5) Teach yourself to identify at least four different cloud-shapes: cirrus, cumulonimbus, etc. Sketch them! (6) Make a sunset report: even if you can't catch the sunset from where you live, look up your town's estimate for sunset and describe what you see outside during that crepuscular moment. What do you hear at sunset? What do you smell? How about at sunrise?

WRITE ABOUT THE MONTH YOU'RE IN NOW. What comes to mind when you think about it / this season? Draw from memories, the five senses, seasonal activities.

FIND A TREE THAT CATCHES YOUR EYE AND WRITE A POEM ABOUT IT. Try to figure out what kind it is if you don't know, using field guides or a tree ID website. Think about what season it is in and describe in excruciating detail what it looks like (are there leaves / blossoms / bare branches)? Think about where you are in relation to it (sat underneath it, looking at it from a passing car, walking up a hill toward it). See where the poem takes you.

WRITE ABOUT A BONFIRE OR A FIREPLACE. Are you someone who loves the smell of fire, and how it lingers on your clothes afterwards? Or someone who hates that the smoke gets in your eyes but you have to get really close to the fire if you want to escape the surrounding cold? Write about how fire warms you and helps people share stories. Why do you think this happens? What is it about fire?

WRITE ABOUT WATER. The ocean, drinking a glass of water, washing yourself or the dishes, the rain. If you choose a body of water, look up a bird that lives there that you didn't know before. What did you learn about this water bird?

WHAT FOOD OR DRINK SENDS YOU IMMEDIATELY BACK TO CHILDHOOD, NO MATTER WHERE YOU ARE? Write about it for about five pages, maximum: *why* it captures your childhood, and see if there are any connections to your present day. Do some research on this food—try to learn more about the folklore and natural history of this food too. Let us smell, feel, taste, hear, and see what it is like to eat/drink it!

TRY GROWING YOUR OWN FOOD OR HERB—SOMETHING YOU'VE NEVER GROWN BEFORE—AND TAKE NOTES! Use a pot and a well-lit window if you don't have access to a garden plot. Write two to three journal entries a week tracking the progress of what you grow. If it doesn't work out, try another herb! Tomatoes and strawberries work great in pots! Basil and parsley grow easily for herbs!

Even *More* Wonders: An Afterword

By popular demand, (in no particular order) these animals and plants are just some of the over 200 wonders
I wanted to write about, but it was near impossible as
the list was ever-changing and evolving and also as the
years (and a pandemic!) went on, it was harder to stay
away from my charming husband and witty kids (who
are now teens!). Also, my eldest will be looking at col-
leges soon and I'm so grateful I gathered up these essays when my boys were still small enough I could still
carry them. But as it often gets asked of me—here's a
few more curiosities in case you would like to explore
these wonders on your own:

1. Blanket octopus
2. Pink robins
3. Rainbow eucalyptus tree
4. Basket star
5. Passion flower
6. Greenland shark
7. Dahlia
8. Painted bunting
9. Humuhumunukunukuāpuaʻa
10. Datura

Music can be a time machine so often for us, right? Anything from Culture Club to Prince to Whitney Houston to The Cure to Dolly Parton, I can just be transported to the first times I heard those hits. That's one of the beautiful things about music and the best kinds of writing—you can feel like you've traveled without ever leaving your couch. For my essays about childhood, I listened to my 70s and 80s soundtrack because there's something about 70s yacht rock and the synthesizer pop of the 80s and 90s R&B that can conjure up those feelings instantly. And music videos, too. Music videos were my window out of my small towns—and they were so expansive, so wide for us.

Also, I never saw anyone bring in pop culture in writing about the outdoors. I read so many books, but I rarely saw anybody who was a mother either, and if I did see a mother, it was someone—no judgment—who some might call "Granola," with Birkenstocks and no makeup. But where were the people who loved the outdoors *and also* makeup and pop music and had crushes? I wanted to show in *World of Wonders* that you can be your full authentic, true self on the page *and* still have some knowledge about flowers, plants, rocks, and crystals. I'm grateful we don't have to choose to have one interest now; I know that wasn't always the case. People didn't make it easy for women to be outdoors without home obligations, for example. But we're not in the 1950s anymore so our writing about the outdoors should reflect that.

By the way, I wrote *World of Wonders* to my boys—I didn't know it would even be published. It was a bedtime storybook, essentially, for them. They would think it was weird if they didn't show up in these essays as we have spent so much time together—and if the vibrant, hot mess that is their mother wasn't also in there. I listen to pop music, I make mistakes, and I love the outdoors. I'm very conscious of including those bits of me personally in there so they could see a record of their mother and see her *outside*. I never saw people who looked like me spending time outside in books.

I was once asked how and why I can write about beauty and joy during dark times. I guess it is rather an *insistence* on finding the light. And it is most definitely work—though my pals would absolutely say I'm an optimist, my very closest loves know I'm a worrier and over-thinker, especially in light of the political and environmental concerns we've been facing. But this is nothing new.

As a woman of color, I have known for a very long time that the world operates very differently for me than say, my white husband. Add that to us raising two half-Asian boys who have some of the most kind and wondrous hearts I know and even though I have an overwhelming sense of dread and despair most days for the world they will live in when I am long gone—it is even more imperative for me to point out beauty and to encourage their curiosity, and yes, joy on this planet for them.

This doesn't, however, mean that I ignore darkness and "scary" topics in my writing. But I suppose I do *try* to lean toward light. I think for many people, it's more helpful to fight for things we love, rather than out of a reflex of fear. So when I turn toward joy and beauty and wonder sometimes in my writing, it is most certainly *work*. But it's the most beautiful and important responsibility in work I've ever had.

And I know it sounds corny as can be but it's frankly so rare to ever see this in a book about nature, let alone any book, so let me say it plain: I actually *like* my family. I adore spending time with my husband, in fact, and of course I love them all, but to actually *like* your family? That takes work. Lots of good, hard work. And in summers, there are fruit pies to be made, and my ageing parents to hang out with, beloved students to guide, my geriatric chihuahua loves walks and cuddles, my beloved pals wanted to travel, gardens needed tending . . . you know: life happens! Good Work happens! Which is what should be occurring when there are so many curiosities and wonders on this planet to marvel over.

My heart is bursting and full of appreciation for the whole team at Milkweed, especially Yanna, Mary, Bailey, and Shannon. The booksellers, educators, readers, students, and people who took a chance on this book during one of the most difficult publishing years in recent memory—you gave this book legs and legs—a most magnificent millipede scurrying along. Thank you for your wonderment. Thank you for taking the time with these pages. You make me want to (like the cassowary) let out a big *boom!* Boom!

TEACHING GUIDE

Selected Common Read Programs

University of Mississippi Common Read
Yale School of the Environment Orientation Selection
Nevada Reads Program
Indiana One State / One Story
Fort Collins Reads
Western Kentucky Community College One Book
Rosemary Choate University All School Read
Sierra Nevada University
Yale School of the Environment
Purdue University Northwest
Centenary College of Louisiana
West Kentucky Community and Technical College

World of Wonders has been adopted for several University First-Year and Honors Seminars, as well as elementary, middle, and high school programs and classes. Courses include Creative Writing, Ethnobotany, Environmental Justice, Creative Nonfiction Workshops, Ecocriticism, Environmental Literature, Human Identity and the Natural World, Literary Landscapes, Environmental Studies, Personal Essay and Memoir, and Environmentalism and the Anthropocene.

Suggested Middle and High School
Essay Prompts

1. Pre-Reading Question: What has surprised you in the natural world? Think of something tht you learned in school, or on your own, that really changed your perception of something in the natural world. This could also be something you were unaware of, or something you were just uninformed of.

2. Based on the "Cactus Wren" essay: What is a "latch-key kid" and what did the author and the rest of the "cul-de-sac of kids" fear? How does the saguaro "stand guard" physically and metaphorically? We have learned a good deal about the author's mother and siblings, but not much about her father thus far. What do we learn about the author's relationship with her father in this essay?

3. Based on the "Narwhal" essay: Why does the author wish she was a narwhal in Kansas? What are at least two unique features of the narwhal's tooth? At the end of the chapter, how does the author compare her family to a pod of narwhals?

4. Based on the "Axolotl" essay: In what ways does the author relate to and learn from the axolotl? Does the axolotl truly "smile"? How does the author highlight some of the less "serene" aspects of the species in the second half of the essay?

5. Based on the "Potoo" essay: When would you say is a time that you feel most "seen," for who you are? When you need to "slow down," or "be still," what do you find helps you? What benefit can come from doing less, being still, looking inward, or taking a step back?

6. Final Essay: Do your own research on an animal or plant in nature and craft a personal essay that connects your own life to something about that plant or animal, while also paying careful attention to narrative and figurative language.

Special thanks to Ms. Leah Umansky, Director of the Scholars Program at York Preparatory School; Ms. Cristina Verasan, science teacher; and Mr. Cliff Burke, English teacher and writer at the Nueva School

More of Ms. Verasan and Mr. Burke's science and English curriculum specifically designed for World of Wonders can be found at milkweed.org

Further Discussion Questions

1. Nezhukumatathil describes wonder this way: "[I]t takes a bit of patience, and it takes putting yourself in the right place at the right time. It requires that we be curious enough to forgo our small distractions in order to find the *world*" (56). How do the essays in this book exemplify her description of wonder? Is everything in the natural world a wonder? What's your personal definition of wonder?

2. The subtitle of the book is "In Praise of Fireflies, Whale Sharks, and Other Astonishments." Why use the word "astonishment"? What does it mean to be "astonished" by something? Does the word imply more about the "astonishing" item or the person who is "astonished" by it? What "astonishes" you in the world?

3. The book begins and ends in Mississippi. What impressions about Mississippi might readers take away from the book? How can writing shape readers' understanding of place?

4. In "Corpse Flower," Nezhukumatathil describes how she tracked blooming corpse flowers for three years.

Why do you think she devoted so much time to that trek? What is it about that particular plant that inspires such fascination? What is it about anything that inspires devoted attention and research?

5. A *Star-Tribune* reviewer says about the book: "Its words are beautiful, but its cover and interior illustrations by Fumi Mini Nakamura may well be what first moves you to pick it up in a bookstore or online." Do you agree? What is so arresting about the images? How do images and text work together to enhance a work?

6. *World of Wonders* speaks to the beauty and surprise of the natural world, along with the responsibility we hold toward it; Nezhukumatathil emphasizes the dangers facing nature as she wrestles with humanity's impact on it. Where does her concern stem from? In what ways do you connect with her message?

7. There is a quality of nostalgia and reflection to World of Wonders. What memories resonate with you? As Nezhukumatathil reflects, what does she learn about herself?

8. From her parents teaching her about fireflies to being a professor at the University of Mississippi,

Nezhukumatathil's life is highlighted with her dedication to education. How does this dedication translate in her writing?

9. Motherhood is a prominent theme in *World of Wonders*. Historically speaking, this has been rare in publishing nature narratives. Too often we hear of someone outside but solitary, and if they are a parent, almost no mention of interacting with children or a partner. In light of this, why do you think Nezhukumatathil included members of her family outdoors? Why do you think she often mentions her "brown skin" and the fact that she is Asian American? What is the connection being made between Nezhukumatathil's experience as a mother and the call to protection she feels for her children and the world around her? Prior to reading this book, how would you describe what a woman enjoying the outdoors looks like? How does your picture change (if at all) after reading this book?

10. A reviewer described Nezhukumatathil's tone this way: "She doesn't scold her readers, but instead asks tender questions: when was the last time you cut a rug like some superb bird of paradise? Or stopped to notice the difference between an oak leaf and a maple leaf?" In addition to asking these questions, how else does Nezhukumatathil avoid a scolding tone in her writing?

Why might her tone be more effective than a reproachful one?

11. Nezhukumatathil moved from one place to another, migrating across the United States, much like the monarch butterflies she writes about. What has this taught her about the importance of home, and what does it teach you?

Adapted from the University of Mississippi Common Read Resource Guide for World of Wonders, with special thanks to Dr. Stephen Monroe and authors Karen Forgette and Guy Krueger from the Department of Writing and Rhetoric.

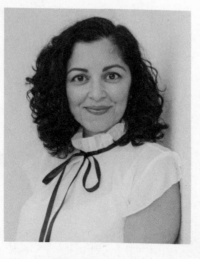

AIMEE NEZHUKUMATATHIL is the author of four collections of poems and poetry editor of *SIERRA*, the national magazine of the Sierra Club. Awards for her writing include fellowships from the National Endowment for the Arts and the Guggenheim Foundation. Her writing has appeared in the *Paris Review, New York Times Magazine,* and *ESPN Magazine,* and twice in *Best American Poetry.* She is professor of English and creative writing in the University of Mississippi's MFA program.

FUMI MINI NAKAMURA is an artist and illustrator based in New York City, and is represented by Thinkspace Art Projects in Los Angeles. She has been commissioned to produce original work for numerous commercial clients including *Harper's Magazine*, Puma, GAP, Dior, Urban Outfitters, and the Cornucopia Institute.

milkweed
EDITIONS

Founded as a nonprofit organization in 1980,
Milkweed Editions is an independent publisher.
Our mission is to identify, nurture, and publish
transformative literature, and build
an engaged community around it.

Milkweed Editions is based in Bdé Óta Othúŋwe
(Minneapolis) within Mní Sota Makhóčhe, the
traditional homeland of the Dakhóta people. Residing
here since time immemorial, Dakhóta people still
call Mní Sota Makhóčhe home, with four federally
recognized Dakhóta nations and many more Dakhóta
people residing in what is now the state of Minnesota.
Due to continued legacies of colonization, genocide, and
forced removal, generations of Dakhóta people remain
disenfranchised from their traditional homeland.
Presently, Mní Sota Makhóčhe has become a refuge
and home for many Indigenous nations and peoples,
including seven federally recognized Ojibwe nations.
We humbly encourage our readers to reflect upon the
historical legacies held in the lands they occupy.

milkweed.org

Milkweed Editions, an independent nonprofit literary publisher, gratefully acknowledges sustaining support from our board of directors, the McKnight Foundation, the National Endowment for the Arts, and many generous contributions from foundations, corporations, and thousands of individuals—our readers. This activity is made possible by the voters of Minnesota through a Minnesota State Arts Board Operating Support grant, thanks to a legislative appropriation from the arts and cultural heritage fund.

Interior design & typesetting by Mary Austin Speaker
Typeset in Essones

Released in 2015, Essones was designed by James
Hultquist-Todd, a former bespoke tailor,
for the P22 Type Foundry.